# The Silver Prescription

# The Silver Prescription

## The Eight-Step Action Plan for Entrepreneurial Success

*A. David Silver*

**JOHN WILEY & SONS**

New York    Chichester    Brisbane    Toronto    Singapore

This publication is designed to provide accurate and
authoritative information in regard to the subject
matter covered. It is sold with the understanding that
the publisher is not engaged in rendering legal, accounting,
or other professional service. If legal advice or other
expert assistance is required, the services of a competent
professional person should be sought. *From a Declaration
of Principles jointly adopted by a Committee of the
American Bar Association and a Committee of Publishers.*

**Library of Congress Cataloging-in-Publication Data:**

Silver, A. David (Aaron David), 1941–
    The Silver prescription—The eight-step action plan
for entrepreneurial success.

    Bibliography: p.
    Includes index.
    1. New business enterprises.   2. Entrepreneur.
I. Title.

HD62.5.S557   1987        658.1'1        86-28135
ISBN 0-471-85637-1

Printed in the United States of America

10 9 8 7 6 5 4 3 2 1

*To George J. Stigler*

# *Preface*

On a warm day in June several years ago, entrepreneur Eugene Lang stepped up to the podium to deliver the commencement address at P.S. 21 in East Harlem, the school Lang had attended as a child. He did not tell the sixty-one graduating sixth graders to go forth with courage on the road of life. He did not assure them they would succeed with hard work and perseverance. He did not inspire them with quotations from the Founding Fathers. Instead, Eugene Lang told them he would pay their college tuition.

And he didn't stop there. He hired Johnny Rivera to run a tutoring program in East Harlem to provide enrichment for the children and to prepare them for the Scholastic Aptitude Test. Lang also kept in touch with the kids, spent time with them, invited them to visit him in the Manhattan offices of his company, Refac Technology Development Corporation. All the kids had to do to earn Lang's gift was stay in school and do well enough to be accepted by a college.

Of the sixty-one P.S. 21 graduates, nine have moved away or dropped out. The remaining fifty-two have stayed in school and in 1986–1987 were in the twelfth grade. All of them were doing well enough to qualify for college. Fifty-two college candidates out of a class of sixty-one would be a remarkable record for any school. For a school in East Harlem, it is astonishing.

Lang is everything an entrepreneur should be. He has spent his life helping people, solving their problems, giving to them. He founded his company, Refac Technology, to help U.S. inventors license their technology abroad and to assist others in bringing foreign inventions to this country. In other words, he identified a large problem, created an elegant solution to it, created a company to convey the solution to the problem, and thereby generated great wealth, which he used to help others, including the kids from P.S. 21.

And that's what this book is about: entrepreneuring successfully—achieving wealth by providing solutions to people's problems and thereby creating employment, stimulating innovation, and reinvesting the wealth in the dreams of others. This book is your guide to the field. Through it you can learn to be a successful entrepreneur.

Entrepreneuring is no longer a mystical field understood by only a handful of unusually gifted individuals. It has evolved into a discipline that can be learned—despite the tendency of some economists to regard it as a mythical kingdom populated by fanatical risk takers who operate on energy and instinct alone. "Entrepreneurship is genetic," the economics professors will say. "It isn't a discipline. Entrepreneurs are born, not made."

I believe those economists are wrong. It's clear to me that entrepreneurship *is* a discipline. It stands somewhere between a science and a game; you can learn to play it, and if you abide by the rules set out in *The Silver Prescription,* you can win.

This notion that entrepreneurship is some kind of an art form has caused the teaching of entrepreneurship to be neglected. That is the problem I will address in this book. I will show you what you need to know in order to play this science-game successfully. I'll take you through its rules, show you how to think like a winning entrepreneur, and give you examples of the way the game has been played. I will start by showing you in detail how an entrepreneur would look at certain real-life situations. I will also discuss the process through which I believe the first entrepreneurs got started. Then I'll list for you the character traits a successful entrepreneur must have and the kinds of leverage that are available to him or her. Later on, we will discuss three basic laws that govern the process of entrepreneurship:

1. The first law of entrepreneurship: Valuation (or "wealth") equals the size of the problem times the elegance of the solution times the excellence of the entrepreneurial team, or $V = P \times S \times E$.

2. The law of the big *P*: It is possible to achieve a high valuation before delivering a solution if the problem to be addressed is very large.

3. The law of risk aversion: Successful entrepreneurs are risk-averse: they hire a team of experienced corporate achievers to manage the operational aspects of the company, leaving the entrepreneur free to handle research and development and manufacturing start-up.

These three laws proscribe the entrepreneurial science-game and state the bases on which it stands: the creation of elegant solutions to big problems, the building of a crack entrepreneurial team, and as a result, the creation of a large valuation.

We will also discuss the fundamentals of the science-game of entrepreneurship:

1. *The GEOs.* By choosing one of the five generic entrepreneurial opportunities, or GEOs, you will be deciding what kind of entrepreneurial problem you wish to solve.

2. *The DEJ Factors.* These are the demonstrable economic justification factors for your company. If you have all eight DEJ factors, you are in shape to win. If you have less than six, you're in trouble before you take the field.

3. *The SDMs.* SDM stands for solution delivery method. It is the means you will use to present your solution to the people whose problem you have set out to solve. There are twelve SDMs; you can choose one or a combination of several.

These fundamentals are spelled out in this guide and illustrated with stories of entrepreneurs who have used them.

When you have a clear understanding of the entrepreneurial process, we will analyze some of the problems people face in today's world, and we'll come up with entrepreneurial solutions for them. We will do this by outlining each problem and solution in accordance with the fundamentals laid out in earlier sections, and we'll discuss some skill-enhancement techniques along the way, including the PERT chart, a valuable start-up tool. Then, in Chapter Nine, I will provide a detailed launch plan that you can use in your own entrepreneurial start-up.

All of the requirements, laws, rules, and fundamentals of entrepreneurship are liberally illustrated with examples of men and women who have already done the things you are now learning to do. Each example makes clear that successful entrepreneurs are people who, like Eugene

Lang, spend their lives giving things to other people. They are altruists at heart. Unlike the dedicated corporate achievers, who are basically egotists working toward their own rise to the top, entrepreneurs have a need to help others—by providing employment, for example, or workable, affordable solutions to serious problems. As a result, entrepreneurs become frustrated with their corporate employers, and thus they decide to leave and start their own problem-solving enterprises.

If you have become disheartened with corporate life, if you have decided to leave your present job and establish your own enterprise, then it is at this point that you need a step-by-step guide to the entrepreneurial process. *The Silver Prescription* can be your bible.

A. DAVID SILVER

*Santa Fe, New Mexico*
*January 1987*

# Acknowledgments

The idea for *The Silver Prescription* came from Jack Gould, Dean of The University of Chicago Graduate School of Business, who challenged me with the statement, "If you think entrepreneurship is a discipline, then prove it. Write the prescription in a way that we can teach it and our students can learn it." Professor Stigler, to whom the result of Dean Gould's challenge is dedicated, taught me how to look at the world in terms of markets twenty years ago. *The Silver Prescription* is my extension of the Stiglerian view of the world.

Credit is also due my partner, Jesse L. Acker, who knows more about launching entrepreneurial companies in the health care market than anyone in the United States. Having brought forth two fine caring and curing companies of his own design, Jesse now tutors entrepreneurs on the subject.

Donna Davis contributed to the text, Eric Beckson assisted with the business plans and Dorothy Moore processed my handwriting. My editor at John Wiley & Sons, Inc., Michael J. Hamilton, made numerous valuable suggestions. Marilyn Dibbs, his assistant, contributed to the final product in many ways.

As a venture capitalist and entrepreneur, I have less time than most authors to write books. The time that I borrow is loaned by my family, Jerilyn, Claude and Caleb. I am eternally grateful to them for providing this most precious of assets and for their continual encouragement.

A.D.S.

# Contents

# The Silver Prescription

# 1

## How to Think like an Entrepreneur

### ENTREPRENEURIAL VISION

Entrepreneurs see life as a huge marketplace. They have, or they develop, an ability to look around them and see opportunities everywhere. In any situation involving two or more people, they see that one person has a problem which the other one might be able to solve. In other words, they view one person as a giver, the other as a receiver. This is entrepreneurial vision—the ability to size up a situation, isolate the problems that exist, devise solutions to them, and then deliver those solutions swiftly and effectively.

Let's go through four perfectly ordinary experiences to see how an entrepreneur would view them.

### Moviegoing

The next time you go to the movies, try to look at the experience through entrepreneurial eyes. See more than the story being played out on the screen. View the star or the director as a source of leverage with which you might be able to raise the capital to produce an independent feature of your own. Also read the credits to find out if the movie was distributed by a large corporation. What about the theater in which the movie is being shown? Is it part of a national chain? Would it be to your advantage to release your future independent feature through such a chain?

Once you have trained yourself to think like an entrepreneur, many everyday experiences, like going to a movie, will become sources of ideas for the future.

### Going through Your Mail

How many pieces of third-class mail did you receive today? How many catalogs? Each item came to you from a company that has your name and address. Those companies got that information by renting mailing lists from firms with which you have done business in the past. As an entrepreneur, can you put this technique to work for your own company? Could you, for instance, begin by renting someone else's list? When you've developed your own roll of customers, could you rent their names and addresses to others in order to generate extra revenue for your company?

### Helping Your Children with Their Homework

You suddenly have a problem: you've forgotten a good many of the details your children need to know. Your entrepreneurial insight should show you several opportunities in this situation. Is there, for example, a market for a certain type of educational software that would solve this problem? Could the problem be solved for a wider number of people by publishing the necessary information in printed form?

### Recovering from an Illness

It happens to everyone once in a while—even the usually healthy entrepreneur: we get flattened for a few days by a flu bug, a killer cold, a ski injury, or some other bothersome ailment. When this happens, the nonentrepreneurial sufferer will take a couple of days off, drink a lot of orange juice, watch television, and indulge in self-pity—but not you! If you have the kind of vision I'm talking about here, or if you are trying to develop that insight, you will look at every angle of the situation through entrepreneurial eyes. How could you improve the lot of those who suffer from the common cold? The first thing that will come to mind is a pharmaceutical solution. Could you develop one entrepreneurially? If you are not pharmaceutically inclined, could you develop and market a nourishing but easy-to-prepare food product designed for easy consumption in the sickroom? A more comfortable pair of crutches for injured skiers? A communications system to connect the sickroom to an office or a classroom?

Something very much like this happened to Charles William Post, who later founded General Foods Corporation. Post fell ill when he was in his thirties. During a stay in a sanitarium in Battle Creek, Michigan, he was served a cereal-based beverage and a breakfast food composed of grain and dried fruits. His depleted physical condition did not prevent him from seeing the sanitarium's menu through the eyes of an entrepreneur. Soon after his release, Post developed his own version of the cereal drink, which he named Monk's Brew at first, and advertised it as a "builder of red blood." After Post changed the product name to Postum, it became a virtual staple product in many American households. The granola–dried fruit cereal became Post's Grape-Nut Flakes, another top seller, but Post didn't stop there. His brief illness had given him still another entrepreneurial idea: a second nourishing breakfast food made from flakes of corn, which he called Post Toasties. From this granola-sized idea was born General Foods Corporation. All that from a short stay in a local sanitarium, and all because Post never for a moment stopped seeing the world through entrepreneurial eyes.

## Watching a Stand-up Comedian

Humor is often based on frustrating problems that could be solved entrepreneurially. A comic, for example, may deliver a routine about trying to put together a bookcase that arrived unassembled. As an entrepreneur, you'll see an opportunity in that problem: people need affordable household items that can be assembled with ease.

Watch "The Tonight Show" for a few nights, and write down the topics that Johnny Carson jokes about during his monologue. In a week you will have a list of ten to twenty entrepreneurial ideas.

## EXERCISING YOUR ENTREPRENEURIAL MUSCLES

The sooner you learn to think entrepreneurially, the better your chances will be of succeeding in this field. Entrepreneurship is a discipline that can be learned. But it takes training. If you weren't "born with it," you can now start nurturing it by exercising your entrepreneurial muscles every day. When you read your morning paper, look at the problems catalogued in every column. Don't throw up your hands in helpless pity. Instead, think up ways to solve those problems entrepreneurially. They don't all have to be solutions that you yourself could provide, or would even wish to provide. They will serve as exercises to enhance your instincts and sharpen your entrepreneurial vision.

Here is what I mean by looking at the world entrepreneurially. Look at big problems of any description and think in terms of their solutions. Here are some big problems. I'm going to give you my own suggestions for solving them. Can you come up with solutions you like better?

## Israel

The nation of Israel is the most passionately entrepreneurial country in the world. It has been fighting for its survival since it was born in fire and flames in 1948. Flanked by enemies who would love to "blow it off the planet," Israel has developed a strong defense establishment and a policy of taking an eye for an eye.

Unfortunately, Israel is broke. It borrows $5 billion to $10 billion per year, depending on how much fighting it did in the previous year. It cannot continue to live with so much of its resources devoted to transfer payments: payments by the government for nonproductive services—services that do not create employment or productivity, such as pensions, immigration allowances, settlements, imports—because triple-digit inflation, high taxes, and constant wars will eventually break Israel's back.

Entrepreneurship marks a stage in the evolution of a person, from childhood selfishness to maturity. It does not last very long because the pace is exhausting and because failure means the entrepreneur may have to return to work for someone else, while dollars mean wealth and a change in one's life from asset building to asset managing. The period of entrepreneurship normally lasts between three and seven years. If it lasts much beyond seven years an entrepreneurial company will normally merge into a larger company.

It is time for Israel to merge. It has been entrepreneurial for thirty-eight years, and the road is just as steep today as it was in 1948. It should merge with another democratic nation that could benefit from Israel's innovations in agriculture, electronics, and health sciences. In return, the other nation could provide Israel with a large army, more capital for investment, and a larger population to buy its goods and services.

Although the pride of government leaders would surely prevent it, I recommend a French-Israeli merger. This would be a classic case: a once-entrepreneurial nation with a population of fifty million would acquire an entrepreneurial nation of three million to get its heart back.

## Artists

Or how about solving a big problem for artists? Unlike musicians who receive a royalty each time their music is played on the radio, sold in a record store, or sold as sheet music, painters and sculptors receive but one payment: when their work is sold for the first time to a collector. Shouldn't artists receive royalties on resales? A possible entrepreneurial solution would be to implant a microchip transmitter on each painting or sculpture and implant a receiver on the telephone line near the front door of the purchaser's home. When the work of art moves out the door (presumably to be sold to another collector) the telephone rings at the entrepreneurial company signalling a transfer of the art and the transferor, by prior agreement, pays a commission to the company which then pays the artist a royalty, or part of the commission. The collector would be willing to do this because it is in his best interest to see that his favorite artists continue to be economically self-sufficient.

Flex your entrepreneurial muscles on some other problems. They can be local, national, or international; you may learn about them firsthand or through newspaper and television reports. Figure out some way to solve each of these problems. And remember, these will not necessarily be solutions you intend to put into action. These are simply exercises to tone up your entrepreneurial muscles and help you to develop an ability to see the world in terms of soluble problems.

Let's look at some other real-life situations through entrepreneurial eyes.

## The Service Economy

Several keen observers of the American scene have reported that America is becoming a service society. More than fifty percent of the nation's gross national product comes from the sale of services rather than products. The principal product of New York City was clothing prior to 1980. Now it is legal services. There were twenty-four more medical schools in the United States in 1980 than there were in 1970. There are more accountants, therapists, consultants, advertising agents, securities analysts, and publicists today than there were ten years ago, and there will be even more ten years from now. What is the reason for these changes?

The products of many American companies have declined in value relative to similar products offered by companies in other countries. Steel, automobiles, consumer electronic products, motorcycles, wine, and many other goods can be produced less expensively in Japan, West

Germany, South Korea, and France. Because these goods can then be sold at a lower price, they outsell many American-made products.

Concomitant with this change, American society has grown more complicated and emotionally stressful for many people. As a result, a need has arisen for therapists of various sorts—people who are trained to solve the problems of stress, stepparenting, chemical abuse, divorce, to name a few. The coping mechanisms that these therapists devise are marketed in a variety of forms: one-on-one office sessions, magazine articles, books, newsletters, software packages, videocassettes, and audio cassettes. This smorgasbord of solutions is the gift of the service economy.

This shift from manufactured products to services illustrates the flexibility of the entrepreneurial mind, a characteristic you will want to cultivate. Examine the marketplace to see where people's needs lie. Did you hope to produce a $40 toaster and then learn that the Japanese are turning out a better one for $17.95? If so, you were addressing a problem that had already been solved by someone else. The only thing to do is pull back, start over, and reexamine that marketplace, perhaps casting your eyes toward the service sector.

## Organized Crime

Organized crime can also be understood from an entrepreneurial point of view. When Eastern European immigrants were filling the large eastern cities of the United States in the late nineteenth and twentieth centuries, a number of them conceived the notion of selling protection. We have seen this in elementary schools. A bully will say to a scrawny wimp of a kid, "Pay me twenty-five cents a day and I'll make sure nobody beats you up."

The scrawny little kid protests that twenty-five cents a day is too much.

"Then I'll beat you up myself," says the bully.

"Okay, okay, I'll pay," says the scrawny little kid.

Organized crime used the same technique to frighten immigrants but charged much more than twenty-five cents. They also found that people in service businesses operating alone were the easiest targets. Thus drivers of vans became the scrawny little kids. Inevitably, some of the businesses that conveyed products or services by van—linen supply, garbage removal, jukebox and vending machines, and trucking itself—were taken over.

Awash in cash and being hounded by the Justice Department for income-tax evasion, organized crime had to find ways to hide cash and make income look legitimate. This led to casino management, where millions of dollars in cash could be merged with customers' cash every night. The casinos of Las Vegas and Havana were launched, and when those were sanitized by an arduous Justice Department, other, more destructive enterprises such as drug traffic replaced them.

From its earliest years, organized crime has operated as a tollgate, a principle we will talk more about in a later chapter: it exacts a fee from its "customers" in return for the right to stay in business—in other words, protection money. This distortion of the entrepreneurial process creates problems and then makes people pay for the solution: If you pay me, I won't beat you up. This is entrepreneurship run amok.

## Baseball

There is a correlation between the growing popularity of baseball and the intensification of the entrepreneurial revolution. Baseball is the sport of entrepreneurs. Football, like other sports that are played against a time clock, is the game of corporation managers. In the 1950s and 1960s when corporations were engulfing and devouring everything in sight, when the conglomerate was born and Harold Geneen ruled on high, pro football became very popular. Expansion teams were formed in Denver, Houston, and other cities via acquisition of the teams in the newly founded American Football League. In the more entrepreneurial 1970s and 1980s, two new professional leagues were launched, but both failed.

Large corporations and professional football have a lot in common. The language is definitive, militaristic, and decisive. A long pass is called a *bomb*. When the linebackers decide to crash through at the snap to tackle the quarterback, it is called a *blitz*. If they succeed, it's called a *sack*.

The coach has a bigger role in football games than in baseball, where individual achievement wins or loses games. The slower the sport, it is said, the greater is management's role. Football is a *very* slow sport. In the 1960s and 1970s, Americans lionized management teams. We were taught to revere the all-knowing men at the top and to tie ourselves to their ideas of the future. If we played our position as well as we could, the manager would call the big plays that kept our corporation in the forefront of its industry. We were known by the prestige or lack of it that our corporate employer carried. Our role was to serve blindly and well.

Political assassinations, the civil rights movement, the Watergate scandal, and other events led Americans to reassess their values in the middle 1970s. Flower children and civil rights marchers of the 1960s were unable to sing out of the corporate songbook. The government began to realize that it could not afford the Great Society, and it began downsizing. Two serious economic recessions, in 1974–1976 and 1981, made managers realize the importance of cash and of managing for cash flow rather than profits. Deconglomeration began, with large corporations spinning off acquired subsidiaries and divisions. Leveraged buy-out techniques enabled entrepreneurs and division managers to acquire these subsidiaries and divisions without using any personal resources.

And with the "small is better" trend came the rebirth of baseball. This is the entrepreneur's game. Winning in baseball requires individual achievement, "sacrificing" to move a base runner, cooperating by distracting the pitcher, making a double play, and hitting behind a runner. The words of baseball are softer than the military verbiage of football. The game is played on a *diamond*. The pitcher stands on a *rubber*. The finest batting achievement is the *home run*. The pitchers throw *fast balls, curves, sliders, forkballs,* and *knuckleballs*. The object in baseball is *to come home*.

In baseball there is no clock. The players have many options. Each field is different. There is variety, uniqueness, novelty. Players must be able to hit, run, and field, and pitchers must be able to throw a variety of pitches.

The new corporate takeover mania made possible by advanced leveraged buy-out techniques has borrowed some baseball language. As William Safire wrote in the *New York Times* on October 20, 1985: "A corporation at which a run has been made by investors or predators is said to be *in play* even if it fights off the attack; hence, those who are in the takeover game are *players*."

The real test of what kind of people are attracted to baseball and which breed loves football is to examine who owns the teams. Real estate and oil businessmen tend to buy football teams, whereas entrepreneurs buy baseball teams.

Here are just a few of the oil and real estate men who have acquired football teams:

- Leon Hess (oil), New York Jets
- John deBartolo (real estate), San Francisco 49ers
- Craig Hall (real estate), Dallas Cowboys
- Jack Kent Cooke (real estate), Washington Redskins

And for contrast, here are some of the entrepreneurs who have bought baseball teams:

- Ewing Marion Kauffman (Marion Labs), Kansas City Royals
- Ted Turner (Turner Broadcasting), Atlanta Braves
- Nelson Doubleday (Doubleday Publishing), New York Mets
- Tom McNaughton (Domino's Pizza), Detroit Tigers
- William Farley (Farley Industries), Chicago White Sox
- Raymond A. Kroc (McDonald's Corporation), San Diego Padres

Their happy relationship with baseball shows that there is a bit of the child in entrepreneurs. They are optimistic. They keep their options open. They place their faith in personal achievement rather than in plays called by the manager. They like the variety of different playing fields. They understand the value of sacrificing and cooperating in order to be a winner.

The relationship of baseball to entrepreneurship is not based on precise statistical analysis, nor on correlation analyses between quantitative baseball game attendances and new company formations, or the number of baseball and softball players nationwide and employment in entrepreneurial companies. However, there is enough empirical data to suggest that the growth in aggregate baseball revenues correlates positively with the growth in entrepreneurial company revenues.

Keep training yourself to look at situations from the entrepreneurial point of view, as we've done in this section. Learn to see problems as opportunities for those entrepreneurs who can come up with workable solutions.

Now that you are on your way toward thinking in terms of problems and solutions, let's examine the personal characteristics an entrepreneur must develop.

# 2

## *The Right Stuff*

When Tom Wolfe spoke of having "the right stuff," he was talking about astronauts, but the term applies to entrepreneurs as well. What character traits does the entrepreneur need in order to make a success of a new company? Here they are:

- Heart
- Patience
- Drive
- The ability to cooperate
- Courage
- An understanding of leverage

As we go through those traits one at a time, take stock of your own character to see which ones you already have and which ones you will have to cultivate.

## HEART

The entrepreneur's value system is based on what is in his or her heart. It is not patterned after the shifting, sometimes faddish values of the community. Successful entrepreneurs do not strive merely to gain wealth or power, nor are they driven by fear of failure. The search for wealth and power and the fear of failure are not valid reasons for work. They lack a moral imperative. They are myths blown out of proportion by movies, novels, and advertisements.

The lives of entrepreneurs are focused by the heart, not by the head. The urges of the heart drive them toward whatever goals they have chosen to pursue. Those people who detach the head from the heart work in large corporations or bureaucratic organizations where they apply their intellects to the success of the company and their own vertical ascent within it. They had hearts at one time, of course, but the corporations had them carefully removed. They become frustrated because their work requires them to do the wrong thing occasionally—to keep silent when they should speak up or to stab a co-worker in the back. Entrepreneurs do not have to deal with these frustrations, although they may have endured them earlier in life. Unlike the corporate workers, they no longer "eat their hearts out."

If you are driven by your heart, you will be optimistic. You will be sure that you can beat the competition, particularly the large corporations, because people with heart always beat people without heart. The reason for this is simple: people with heart know what drives people without heart, but people without heart do not know how the people with heart play the game. Thus the people with heart build their unique products and pluck from the large corporations the most intelligent people to join their teams. These new recruits, the corporate achievers, get their hearts back along with some stake in what they are doing, and they "work smart," attacking the weak points of the corporations they know so well.

Entrepreneurial heart makes the difference between the egotistical industrialist and the true altruist who invests his or her profits in the dreams of others. William H. Danforth, who founded Ralston Purina Company, had heart. He was more concerned with helping others than he was with enriching himself, and his altruism took many forms: he instituted a physical fitness program for his employees (and even led them in calisthenics every day), and he funded a workshop to train teachers to work among the American Indians.

Milton Hershey, founder of the Hershey Corporation, founded an orphanage and left his shares of Hershey stock (56 percent) to it when he died. Some $50 million of his wealth went to Penn State University in 1963 to start a medical school.

The Southland Corporation, another entrepreneurial venture with heart, raises about $5 million each year for Jerry Lewis's Labor Day telethon for the Muscular Dystrophy Association.

James W. Rouse is another entrepreneur whose heart drives him to improve the lives of others. His company moves into depressed, ugly urban neighborhoods and turns them into showplaces lined with beautiful shops and clean, affordable housing. Among his accomplishments is the Faneuil Hall Marketplace in Boston. There, in a city neighborhood that was once a depressing eyesore, Rouse created a vital environment that attracts millions of visitors each year. New York's South Street Seaport is also the result of Rouse's entrepreneurial heart. His other projects include Baltimore's Charles Center, a mall in downtown Toledo, and San Francisco's Yerba Buena Gardens, a former skid row that Rouse is renovating to resemble Copenhagen's Tivoli Gardens. "I have a conviction," Rouse says, "that optimism is a value, not a sentimental state of mind. It helps to bring about what ought to be."

## PATIENCE

"The single most important factor in venture capital investing," states Thomas P. Murphy, "is patience." Murphy should know; he is a venture capitalist who for many years wrote a column for *Forbes*. He could have extended his statement to include the entrepreneurs in whom the venture capitalists invest, because they too must develop an abundance of patience.

Why is patience important? Because entrepreneurial enterprises do not provide instant gratification. It takes time to find a problem, develop a solution to it, choose a method of delivering that solution, and put the entrepreneurial process into operation. Only after all of those things have been done—and done right—will gratification materialize. The early American shipping magnates are often cited as an example of the kind of patience an entrepreneur needs. They had to endure long periods of waiting while their ships made the arduous journey to Europe and back. Only after long months, sometimes years, did the ships return with the rewards. Technology has diminished the amount of time between investment and gratification, but even today the entrepreneur needs to be able to wait patiently for the reward.

One entrepreneur who knew the value of patience was Gail Borden.

He invented condensed milk in 1857 when he was fifty-six years old, but it was not until several years later that other people began to see the value of his invention.

Borden had worked as a surveyor, teacher, landowner, cattle rancher, and customs collector. In still another career, journalism, he created one of the most famous headlines in American history—"Remember the Alamo!"—while working for the *Telegraph and Texas Register*. His passion, however, was condensation. "Condense your sermons," he advised his pastor. "The world is changing." Borden became obsessed with the notion that food could be preserved by condensing it. He invented a condensed meat biscuit that was used during the Gold Rush in California. It was nourishing, and it didn't spoil, but neither did it make Borden's fortune— it tasted awful. He also managed to condense potatoes, but again, no one else saw the value of his accomplishment.

Only when the Civil War was in full swing and the armies needed preserved milk, did Borden begin to see profits from his invention. After years of patience, this entrepreneur finally had the last laugh.

You will need another kind of patience to succeed as an entrepreneur: patience with a lack of perfection. Successful entrepreneurs and their investors are not perfectionists. They strive for satisfaction only. Perfection is either unattainable or too costly to achieve. Robert Sind, president of Recovery Management Corporation, an entrepreneurial company that does workouts and turnarounds for the bad loans of commercial banks, says, "In the venture capital business there are no touchdowns. Only the occasional first down to make us cheer. If you hope to get touchdowns, you will be dumped behind the line and have to turn over the ball."

Why have many successful entrepreneurs come from farms or agricultural communities? Perhaps because farming teaches patience, and farmers know all about delayed gratification. They invest large amounts of money and time in sowing their crops at the beginning of the growing season. Only months later, when the crops are harvested and sold, does their reward materialize. In years of drought or unusually low temperatures, the reward may not appear at all, or may be too small to satisfy the farm family's needs. The farmer patiently waits another whole year and then tries again.

Wherever they learned patience—on the farms, from a parent or a mentor, or as a result of an early employment experience—entrepreneurs would be lost without it. Their market research would be done too hastily, their product would leave the laboratory too soon, the marketing effort would be inadequate. Then, when nothing worked right, when the product was shipped back due to bugs, when the critical component suppliers demanded payment in advance, when the bank called the note, when the salespeople quit—all in the same week—the entrepreneur without patience would throw in the towel.

## DRIVE

Between 1967 and 1977, Randall Keith Filer evaluated 4,300 persons in terms of sex, education, salary, cognitive skills, training, profession, occupation, and industry. The personality characteristic that correlated most positively with high earnings in the Filer study was *drive*. Earnings and wealth are different, but achieving either requires drive. Patience can lead to wealth, but not to high earnings; for those you need drive.

It is at least partly because of a lack of drive that relatively few entrepreneurs emerge from the ranks of the very poor or the extremely wealthy. The latter have lost their drive and are merely part of the process of dissipating the remaining wealth of an earlier entrepreneur from whom they inherited their fortunes. The poor, on the other hand, expend so much energy keeping a roof over their heads and food on their tables that they have little drive left to channel into entrepreneurship.

The entrepreneurial spirit exists primarily among people who have grown up in the middle and working class. These people have the drive to keep them moving toward a goal that may at first seem impossibly far away. Unlike the very rich, they have not grown complacent; unlike the extremely poor, they don't need to scramble simply to survive.

Drive seems to have been instilled in some people at an early age, most often by their parents. The frontier-style mother and father, for instance, will raise their children to be strong, self-reliant, energetic, and optimistic. Their offspring learn that good things won't fall from the sky, that they will have to move forward under their own steam in pursuit of what they want. And the parents instill these attitudes in their daughters as well as their sons. "Don't marry a millionaire," the daughter is told. "Become one!"

This kind of drive, whether it is instilled in you by your parents at an early age or developed independently later on, will serve you all your life. Because of it, you will work harder than other people and keep trying for as long as you have to in order to reach that now distant goal.

As an example of drive, I like to tell the story of Henry J. Heinz—who, by the way, also had heart, courage, patience, and all of the other characteristics we are talking about here. He and a business partner began selling bottled foods in 1869 when Heinz was only twenty-five. The business fell victim to the Panic of 1875, however, and Heinz was financially ruined. What happened next serves as a measure not only of his drive but of his tremendous integrity as well. He drew up a list of the people to whom he owed money as a result of his business failure, and he labeled the list "M.O.," for "moral obligations." Then he dug in his heels and set to work, with the immediate goal of repaying every one of his creditors. Having succeeded in that endeavor, he plunged ahead into a new bottled-foods venture. He called his new company H. J. Heinz, Inc. Instead of stopping or slowing down when his first products brought him success and wealth, Heinz let his drive take him further and further forward until, at the end of the nineteenth century, his entrepreneurial enterprise was one of the premier businesses of the day. Even now the company dominates the ketchup, pickle, and mustard markets.

## THE ABILITY TO COOPERATE

No entrepreneur works in a vacuum. If you enter this field, you will be in contact with other people almost constantly: venture capitalists, vendors, key employees, clients, and many others. Your venture will not succeed unless you can cooperate, or learn to cooperate, with them and at the same time persuade them to cooperate with you. It takes two, after all, to cooperate.

The best way to ensure cooperation is to prepare a written statement of your company's mission very early in the game. Clearly state the goals toward which you will be working and the moral code by which you will operate. Ask the people you hire to read this statement carefully. Tell them that they will be happy at the company only if they respect the mission and abide by the code of ethics. Clarity is vital to cooperation. People cannot cooperate with you unless they know exactly what you want from them and what you will not tolerate. Therefore, it is important to make yourself clear. Let others know what you expect of them, and what they can expect from you.

The great enforcer of cooperation in the entrepreneurial company is the continuing relationship. You and the others are bound together through ownership of a significant amount of the company's stock; you must cooperate with one another if you want that stock to increase in value. At the same time, you are bound to suppliers and customers by the law of reciprocity: the understanding that you and the suppliers and the customers will have to keep exchanging commodities in order to succeed. When someone fails to reciprocate, he or she loses out.

The bonds of cooperation are not so tight in a large corporation. There, many employees refuse to cooperate. They may, for example, take credit that is due to a co-worker. Or they might fail to reciprocate after another employee cooperates with them. Many corporate people neglect to explain clearly exactly what they expect from others in the organization; the result of this lack of clarity is often a failure of cooperation or a misunderstanding about ethical standards. Confusion can result. At that point, the potential entrepreneur—frustrated and disappointed by the corporation—departs to form a company in which cooperation will always be reciprocated.

Masaru Ibuka and Akio Morita understood the importance of cooperation back in 1948 when they founded the SONY Corporation. They even wrote the words "mutual cooperation" into the original statement of their company's mission. As the years passed and the company grew, cooperation remained a priority and became recognized as a mark of SONY's operation. Ibuka and Morita cooperated with customers by providing top-quality products, and the customers reciprocated that cooperation by paying higher prices for goods that carried the SONY name—the law of reciprocity in action.

## COURAGE

To succeed as an entrepreneur you will need courage—not the physical sort that is expected of test pilots and submariners, but the courage of your convictions—moral courage. You will have to be brave enough to try something new, to accept criticism without losing heart, to invest your time and money in something before that something even exists, to move into a new marketplace when the time is right, and to do the thousand other things that will be necessary to build a successful enterprise.

The mention of courage again brings to mind the shipping entrepreneurs of earlier years. It must have taken enormous courage for a man to invest his life savings in a cargo that had a good chance of sinking to the bottom of the sea during a storm or being seized by pirates. But the early merchants had that kind of courage, and as a result they became wealthy while providing the goods that other people needed and wanted.

Cecilia Danieli of Italy provides an example of that kind of courage in our own time. When she assumed control of the Danieli Company in 1980, the construction firm was in serious financial trouble. It had losses of 1.7 billion lire, and profit margins were getting thinner and thinner on large construction jobs. She took three bold and courageous steps and, by doing so, not only saved the company but turned it into an enterprise that did 300 billion lire in sales in 1985.

Her first step was to rewrite the company's business plan, a move that meant rethinking the very bases on which Danieli Company was built.

Once that was done, she began bidding on midsize projects only, eschewing the huge jobs. She put her company's energy into turnkey projects, too, in which it was responsible for designing, managing, and commissioning entire factories. The third step in her strategy was to move boldly out beyond Italy to seek jobs in other European countries and even in the Soviet Union and the Eastern bloc nations. To obtain the kind and quantity of revenue she was seeking, Danieli made the sales trips herself. The results included contracts to build a rolling mill in Sweden, a 750,000-ton-a-year steel mill in the U.S.S.R., and a bundling plant in Byelorussia.

Because she had the courage to make moves that no one else had dared to try, Danieli has built her company into a world-class operation that locks horns with Mitsubishi, Hitachi, NKK, and Krupp, and that, too, requires the courage of a lion.

Danieli Company's performance warranted an initial public offering in 1984 at which twenty-six percent of its stock was sold at 2,250 lire per share. The stock currently trades at 10,500 lire per share.

The wellsprings of courage seem also to produce in many individuals a kind of entrepreneurial vision that allows them to look at a problem and see directly through it to a solution that is original, immediate, and satisfactory to all concerned. At age sixteen, in the depths of the Great Depression, Jeno Paulucci, who was to found Chun King Corporation, worked in a Duluth, Minnesota grocery store. One warm day, the store's refrigerator broke down, causing eighteen crates of bananas to develop brown-speckled skin. The bananas were otherwise undamaged, but because of their unusual appearance, the store owner told his young employee to take them outside and sell them at bargain prices. Jeno, however, was a man of courage and vision even at that young age. He took the fruit outside, made a sign saying "Argentine Bananas," and began shouting about the shipment of exotic fruit. Within three hours he had sold all eighteen crates at a price four cents a pound higher than that of ordinary bananas.

A number of entrepreneurs demonstrated physical as well as moral courage on their way to success. Juan Benitez, for instance, escaped from Cuba and made his way to the United States, where he became a plant manager at Mostek. Later, he left the security of that job to become a member of the entrepreneurial team at Micron Technology, Inc.

Philip Hwang escaped from North Korea into the free south when he was only fourteen years old. There he sold pencils to earn money for his education. Later, he arrived at Utah State University with a scholarship and $50 as his total assets. During his first months in Utah he lived on pumpkin pie filling given to him by a minister. The same courage that helped him survive those early years also allowed Hwang to found Tele-Video Systems, a manufacturer of computer terminals, and to retain his clear vision of a plan to turn his company around when the computer industry shake-out crippled his company.

## AN UNDERSTANDING OF LEVERAGE

The final characteristic needed by the entrepreneur is an appreciation for, and understanding of leverage. There are two kinds of leverage— financial and communications. Communications leverage is the ability to persuade people to do things for you that they had no intention of doing until you asked them to. Financial leverage, for our purposes, is the use of borrowed money to start an entrepreneurial company.

Borrowing start-up capital, of course, means going into debt, a reality with which most businesspeople are comfortable. In fact, competent entrepreneurs, as many people have observed, are comfortable incurring more debt than they would be able to repay if they were called on to do so. They are also excellent communicators. In other words, they understand and appreciate both kinds of leverage.

Because this subject is of extreme importance to anyone who plans to launch an entrepreneurial company, leverage is the sole subject of the following chapter.

# 3

# Leverage

## FINANCIAL LEVERAGE

*Debt.* The very word frightens many people, but it should not intimidate the budding entrepreneur. In the absence of inherited or previously earned wealth, there is often no possibility of launching a new company except by incurring debt. Fortunately, numerous alternative methods of obtaining leverage are available, and some of them do not carry a repayment obligation.

The sources of financial leverage are listed here, and a detailed discussion of each method follows:

- Accounts receivable financing
- Government-guaranteed loans
- Grants
- R&D limited partnerships
- Leveraged buy-outs
- Business Development Corporations
- Joint ventures and licensing

- Small Business Investment Companies
- Minority Enterprise Small-Business Investment Companies
- New issues market
- Venture capital funds
- Customer financing

## Accounts Receivable Financing

Commercial finance companies, or asset-based loan divisions of commercial banks, whose business is to make asset-based loans, generally provide accounts receivable financing. Because they understand the assets they lend against and, more important, know where to sell the assets if they have to and at what price, commercial finance companies will frequently make loans to companies that lack positive cash flow or secondary collateral.

Keep three things in mind when you consider using commercial finance companies:

1. *Their Interest Rates Tend to Be High.* These companies do not relend depositors' investments; rather, they borrow at interest rates that average a shade below the prime rate. Their charges range from prime plus two percent to prime plus five percent.
2. *Their Loans Carry Prepayment Penalties.* Knowing that the borrower will leave them at the first opportunity to go with a less expensive lender, these companies build into their loan agreements a prepayment penalty as stiff as one year's interest if the loan is paid off within twelve months or as lenient as two months' interest if the loan is prepaid within six months.
3. *They Generally Prefer the Most Liquid Assets on the Balance Sheet.* They may prefer accounts receivable or finished goods inventory, for example, rather than real property or equipment, unless that is their specialty.

### Government-Guaranteed Loans

Loans guaranteed by the U.S. Small Business Administration (SBA) are available to small businesses in amounts up to $500,000 for seven years, repayable usually in eighty-four equal monthly installments at an interest rate governed by the U.S. Congress, but usually a few points over prime. The higher the interest rate, the more aggressive the lenders. The SBA guarantees ninety percent of the face amount of the loan. Thus the entrepreneur must persuade a commercial bank or SBA-approved lender such as a Business Development Corporation to provide ten percent of the loan. In fact, the lender puts the full amount of the loan in the borrower's bank account and either earns interest on the full amount of the loan or sells the guaranteed portion to a buyer of government-guaranteed loans at a premium. For processing the loan for the secondary buyer, the bank can earn a monitoring fee and a spread between the rate the borrower pays it and the rate it charges in the secondary market. The processing charge is usually around one percent per annum on the total loan; the spread is about half that amount. Couple these charges with its rate on the unguaranteed portion, and you'll see that banks which are active in the SBA guaranteed loan business can earn over fifteen percent per annum on that portion of their loan portfolio.

## Grants

Grant money is available to entrepreneurs from a wide variety of sources, but the grants are not easy to obtain.

The smallest research and development grants are those offered by the National Science Foundation (NSF). The NSF will award $25,000 to an individual for the purpose of conducting original research in an area that NSF believes is socially useful. In recent years, NSF has favored energy-saving projects and research into alternative energy sources. The application for the $25,000 NSF grant is rather lengthy and can be submitted only during a brief period once a year.

The state of Connecticut offers grants of up to $350,000 for the development of a product that could lead to increased employment of scientists in the state.

The large and more interesting grants are those offered by private foundations: Ford, Rockefeller, Kellogg, Carnegie, and other family foundations whose mission is to return to the community in a sensible manner some of the wealth created by entrepreneurs of an earlier age. These entrepreneurs, like Andrew Carnegie, believed that their wealth should be held in trust for the benefit of the country. There are literally thousands of foundations in the United States which are listed in directories, which give their assets, their locations, and the names of key decision-makers.

## R&D Limited Partnerships

Section 174 of the Internal Revenue Act provides that "A taxpayer may treat research or experimental expenditures which are paid or incurred by him during the taxable year in connection with his trade or business as expenses which are not chargeable to capital account. The expenditures so treated shall be allowed as a deduction." The phrase "in connection with his trade or business" was clarified in 1974 when the U.S. Supreme Court held that a new limited partnership organized for the purpose of developing a new process or product is entitled to deduct research and experimentation expenditures. In other words, the investor need not be the manufacturer and need not even be in business to get the tax deduction on research carried out in his or her behalf.

Therefore, an R&D tax shelter is usually organized as a partnership, and the research is typically conducted by a company under contract with the partnership. The same company is most often granted the option to license the technology developed and to manufacture products utilizing the technology. The partnership's remuneration is then tied to the sales of products that result from the research, but there can be no guarantee of remuneration or, for that matter, repurchase of the technology from the partnership, for if there were, the partnership would not be at risk on the research.

Wealthy private investors readily invest in R&D limited partnerships because they are able to reduce their personal income taxes—hence, leverage the Federal government—and possibly achieve a return on their investment in the future if the research and development that their partnership pays for comes up with a useful solution to someone's problem. Genentech, Inc., a biotechnology start-up, raised $50 million via the R&D limited partnership route several years ago to develop genetically-based solutions to the problems of dwarfism and hoof and mouth disease. The research paid off in 1986, and Genentech bought out its partners for $240 million.

## Leveraged Buy-Outs

A leveraged buy-out (LBO) is the purchase of a company, using its assets to secure loans with which to pay the seller. If the assets are inadequate to attract the full sales price, the seller must be persuaded to take promissory notes or the buyer must attract equity capital. Naturally, persuading the seller to take promissory notes to be paid out of his old company's earnings is the preferable route. The more equity capital required, the smaller the percentage of ownership the entrepreneur is able to keep. If the company's asking price is too high or the cost of debt financing too dear, more equity capital will be required, to the point of diluting the entrepreneur's interest. At some point the entrepreneur will have to walk away from the deal.

The best candidates for LBOs are divisional spin-offs from large industrial corporations. These giants periodically go through a housecleaning exercise in which they discard small divisions or subsidiaries appended to larger companies acquired many years earlier when the corporation's goals and objectives were perceived differently. These small divisions are frequently not attractive to other corporations because of their size, thus making them candidates for entrepreneurial purchase. Private or family-owned companies are less attractive leveraged buy-out candidates because the recordkeeping is usually sloppier, and there is no assurance that the family is truly a willing seller. Sometimes they will put their company on the market merely to establish a value for estate-planning purposes. In a divisional spin-off, the board has authorized the president not only to sell but also to get the best price with the greatest amount of cash. Further, the division is usually audited every year, and the key general-ledger items are normally maintained on computer.

## Business Development Corporations

Perhaps the most flexible lenders in the country are the Business Development Corporations (BDCs), which are chartered by twenty-seven states to make loans to small businesses where the end result is job creation. The BDCs are a well-kept secret. Very few entrepreneurs know of their existence, hence they are substantially underutilized.

Curiously, slightly less than half of the states do not have BDCs, and many of the non-BDC states are capital importers with few venture capital funds. The states that have BDCs are Arkansas, California, Florida, Georgia, Iowa, Kansas, Kentucky, Maine, Maryland, Massachusetts, Mississippi, Missouri, Montana, Nebraska, New Hampshire, New Mexico, New York, North Carolina, North Dakota, Oklahoma, Pennsylvania, Rhode Island, South Carolina, Virginia, Washington, West Virginia, and Wyoming.

Some BDCs are owned by a group of private investors who obtain a license from the state; others are owned by financial institutions and large corporations in the state. Funding is generally provided by individual financial institutions and corporations in the state whose interests are served by an increase in the number of available jobs.

## Joint Ventures and Licensing

Joint venturing is frequently overlooked as a source of seed capital and as a method of launching a new company. A joint venture is a partnership of two or more entities, formed to undertake a certain project. A joint venture opportunity exists when each partner brings to the project a property that the other partners do not have but which they regard as integral to the success of the project.

An entrepreneur in search of seed capital must honestly confront the fact that more than money is necessary to launch a new company. Although the project may call for the manufacture or distribution of a certain product, merely obtaining capital does not make the entrepreneur the most efficient manufacturer or the most successful distributor of the product.

Licensing has myriad ramifications. In terms of raising venture capital, however, one should ask certain questions:

- Is there a submarket that is willing to pay a premium for my product because it solves a serious problem?
- Is there an entity in that submarket that can manufacture and market my product?
- Is that entity large enough to pay me a substantial down payment and to guarantee the payment of future minimum royalties?
- What is the potential size of that submarket measured in dollars per annum?
- What is the highest-level contact that I can establish with that entity? (An introduction through an investment or commercial banker is preferred.)

The optimal licensing arrangement involves a substantial down payment by the licensee and relatively high annual minimum sales goals.

## Small Business Investment Companies

Since 1946, the vehicle through which the federal government aids small business has been the Small Business Administration (SBA) of the Department of Commerce. In addition to its government-guaranteed loan program, the SBA provides funds through its Small Business Investment Company (SBIC) program. An SBIC is licensed by the SBA to invest in or make loans to small businesses. The SBIC's owners must show that they have at least $1 million in capital (at the beginning of the SBIC program the amount was $150,000), and the SBA will provide loans to the SBIC of up to 400 percent of available capital.

Because SBICs pay interest to the SBA, they prefer to lend their capital rather than invest it in order to earn an interest greater than the amount they pay out. As a result, SBICs are more interested in companies well beyond the conceptual or start-up stages of their operations.

There are over four hundred SBICs in existence in the United States, with an average capitalization of about $500,000. Some of them will invest in early stage companies, particularly if they are located near the SBIC.

## Minority Enterprise Small Business Investment Companies

The Department of Commerce created a new division of the SBA in 1964 to assist minorities in entering the entrepreneurial process. This division is the Office of Minority Business Enterprise (OMBE). Having participated in some of the early planning sessions in 1966–1967, I am aware of OMBE's purpose and goals. It was created to assist blacks and other minorities in owning businesses in inner cities. As white flight led to urban blight in burned-out downtown areas like those of Detroit and Chicago, OMBE looked for mechanisms by which blacks could own automobile dealerships, retail stores, and fast-food franchises to enhance commerce in rapidly eroding downtown business districts.

The OMBE came up with a stepchild of the SBIC program (which was then in full flower): The Minority Enterprise Small Business Investment Company (MESBIC). To obtain a MESBIC license, the SBA required a net worth of $150,000. It provided investments in MESBIC on a 4-to-1 ratio in the form of preferred stock, with a three percent dividend rate after five years and a twenty-year redemption period.

Many large corporations formed MESBICS—among them Ford Motor Company, General Foods Corporation, and Equitable Life Assurance Company of the United States—and for the first time blacks and other ethnic groups had a special way of obtaining capital. Approximately two hundred MESBIC licenses were granted, and the program was launched at top speed. Unfortunately, the 1974 recession eliminated many minority entrepreneurs whose retail establishments were thinly capitalized, and about two-thirds of the MESBICs collapsed and died. The surviving MESBICs are well capitalized and intelligently managed by experienced investors.

## New Issues Market

The three centers of underwriting activities in the new issues market are Denver, Jersey City, and New York City. The Denver underwriters appear to favor start-up companies and common stocks priced at 25 cents or less. These are commonly referred to as penny stocks. One of the problems associated with penny stocks is getting them up to more than $1 where they will interest national investors. (In fact, Californians are restricted from buying common stocks having initial underwriting prices of less than $3.)

Investors in penny stocks think like slot-machine players in Las Vegas. When the stock they purchased goes from five to fifty cents, they tend to dump it. With this kind of resistance, it is difficult over the near term to get the stock up to an attractive price even when earnings improve. A penny stock issue certainly raises capital, but it may be years before the entrepreneur can pledge this stock as collateral, sell it, or use it to acquire other companies and attract key management.

Favorite issues of the Denver underwriters appear to be oil- and gas-related and high-technology stocks. A spate of penny stock offerings between 1979 and 1981 by Denver underwriters backed geologists in their search for oil. Few endeavors are as risky as oil exploration, but risk is apparently what the investors liked.

Jersey City is a step up in quality of new issue underwritings. Although Jersey City itself has a fair number of small underwriters, the name applies to several regional underwriters in Albany, Philadelphia, and other towns near New York City.

The basic Jersey City new issue offering is a common stock priced from $1 to $2 per share. Whereas the Denver style is to authorize 20 million shares, then issue 8 million to management, 4 million to treasury, and 8 million to the public at 10 cents per share ($800,000 in proceeds), Jersey City typically authorizes two million shares, issues 800,000 to management, and sells 800,000 to the public for $2 per share ($1.6 million in proceeds). The Jersey City underwriters prefer higher quality—an operating history, for example, or an initial investment by the founding entrepreneurs of $20,000 or so.

The qualifications of many of the companies who foist their paper off on an unsophisticated public are extremely weak by many of the standards of entrepreneurial excellence described herein. Yet Xicor Corporation, a successful semiconductor manufacturer, began with a public issue of stock underwritten by D. H. Blair, Inc. in 1982. Control Data Corporation's founding entrepreneur, William C. Norris, raised his initial $1.6 million via a self-underwritten initial public offering marketed in the living rooms of various friends. A handful of other successful companies raised their initial capital with a dollar issue through small regional underwriters.

Across the Hudson River in lower Manhattan is Wall Street where, it has been said, "gentlemen come to raise money." Most of the New York

City underwriters who are inclined to manage new issues will not underwrite start-ups, but that rule is broken frequently. The venerable Allen & Company, early backers of Syntex Corporation, developer of the birth-control pill, raised $5 million in 1981 for Codenol, a start-up laser development company. Goldman, Sachs & Co.—investment banker to Ford Motor Company and the New York Times Company, among others—underwrote a new issue in 1981 for Hybritech Corporation, a monoclonal antibody research and development company that had nominal revenues. In 1985, Hybritech was acquired by the Eli Lilly Company for $300 million.

Wall Street sponsored underwritings have a higher price per share—somewhere between $5 and $20—and the number of shares is correspondingly fewer, with the average offering producing approximately $10 million for the company. Certain new issues can raise more capital if the problem that the company purports to be addressing is large, if the management team is extremely well experienced, or if there are promising aspects such as important contracts, numerous patents, or important customers or suppliers. This happened with Genentech, Inc., a premier biotechnology company that manufactures interferon, a possible cure for several diseases.

## Customer Financing

A substantial number of successful service companies have been customer financed because it occurred to the entrepreneurs that their customers could be persuaded to risk payment up front, thus assuring receipt of the companies' products. The insurance industry, for example, was launched with customer financing. Well-known customer-financed companies include Arthur Murray Dance Studios; Weight Watchers International, Inc.; Century 21 Real Estate, Inc.; EST; Esprit de Corp.; Evelyn Wood Reading Dynamics, Inc.; ComputerLand Corporation; CMP Communications; Renovator's Supply Company; Mary Kay Cosmetics, Inc.; Avon Products; Shaklee Corporation; Time, Inc.; and Maxicare, Inc.

The primary forms of customer financing are the following:

• Franchising

• Facilities management

• Newsletters and seminars

• Direct mail marketing

• Licensing

- Consulting
- Partyplan selling

The advantages of customer financing are that it preserves equity for the entrepreneurial team, it involves the customer directly in developing the solution to the problem, and it is faster than making presentations to investors and their attorneys.

The disadvantage of customer financing is that there must be no delay in delivering the service or product that the customer has paid for in advance. Thus the entrepreneur must prepare the product or service in advance and be ready to deliver it within sixty days of receiving payment.

Society as a whole benefits from this kind of financing because the customer is involved with the development of an appropriate cost-effective solution to a problem. This saves time, and venture capital is conserved for more capital-intensive projects.

## COMMUNICATIONS LEVERAGE

The founder of Businessland, Inc., David Norman, convinced IBM Corporation to license his company as a dealer in IBM Personal Computers before Businessland had opened its first store. IBM has a firm policy against awarding dealerships prior to inspecting locations and ascertaining the financial strength of the proposed dealer. However, Norman was able to convince IBM that if he received their blessing, the financial support would be forthcoming. Indeed it was. Soon thereafter, Businessland raised $76 million from venture capital investors and the public market, much more capital than was raised by the rest of the industry combined.

When Phillip Moffitt and Christopher Whittle founded 13-30 Corporation—publishers of numerous single-sponsor magazines on a facilities-management basis for Kimberly-Clark Corp., Johnson & Johnson, and others—they had no capital to fund their cash flow deficit. At that time, Moffitt and Whittle were students at the University of Tennessee. They persuaded their economics teacher, Tony Spiva, to personally guarantee a line of credit at Valley Bank for them. The loans to 13-30 Corporation quickly grew to $1 million, more than Spiva's net worth.

These entrepreneurs had sufficient faith in their dreams to persuade others to provide them with the support they needed to turn those dreams into reality. But in addition to their belief in themselves, they possessed another entrepreneurial skill: a mastery of communications leverage and a clear understanding of which communication method worked best for them.

Like those three businessmen, you will need to persuade various lenders, suppliers, and investors to place their trust in you. When you talk people into shipping your product on terms, lending you equipment rent free, guaranteeing $1 million in loans, or investing $76 million in your dream, you are leveraging just as surely as if you had borrowed money from a bank. It is important to note, however, that the use of communications leverage does not result in a promise to repay a sum of money on a certain date, with the penalty of foreclosure and litigation if the sum is not repaid. Communications leverage involves negotiating skills and an ability to persuade and to capture the imagination of the other person with the picture of some future reciprocity. Competent entrepreneurs are adept at persuading people to do things for them that they never intended to do.

To gain an understanding of just how they do this, let's take a look at some of the most useful tools in the gentle science of persuasion.

## Communications Leverage Techniques

The techniques of communications leverage, as the other skills needed by the entrepreneur, can be learned, practiced, and perfected. Here is a list of helpful techniques:

- Careful selection of communications medium
- Thorough preparation for the negotiations
- Thoughtful scheduling
- Wise choice of questions
- Awareness of body language
- Awareness of personal style

## Selecting the Communications Medium

Are you at your best when you talk with someone on a one-to-one basis? If so, you should arrange to meet with your target in an office or restaurant where the two of you will be alone together. If, on the other hand, you feel most confident and convincing while chatting with a group of people, then that is the kind of situation in which you should do your communicating.

Some entrepreneurs prefer a less direct form of communication. A strong, persuasive writer, for example, might want to conduct the larger part of the negotiations by letter or memo. Another entrepreneur may feel most comfortable when talking on the telephone. Still others may wish to put this problem in the hands of an advertising agency or a public relations firm.

The medium you choose should be the one in which you are at your most persuasive and in which you feel most comfortable.

## Preparation for the Negotiations

Before you meet with lenders or suppliers, learn as much as possible about their products and services. Also take into consideration all possible outcomes of the negotiations and decide on the one toward which you will work. Review in your mind—or on paper, if you wish—the aspects of your business that will serve best to convince the targets of your proposal to put their faith in you.

Keep in mind, as you prepare for the meeting, that lenders, customers, and suppliers have specific needs and requirements of their own. Know what these are and avoid making requests that would conflict with those needs.

## Scheduling

In negotiations of this sort, having plenty of time is a great advantage. Schedule your meetings with this in mind. Don't crowd together the moment when you ask for something and the moment when you absolutely must have it.

## Wise Choice of Questions

In any discussion, the person who controls the questions controls the power. "Smart is dumb and dumb is smart," says Somers H. White, a communications consultant. "Ask lots of questions to guide the conversation." Spend as much time as necessary beforehand to decide what questions you will ask during the meeting.

## Awareness of Body Language

Be alert to any nonverbal messages the lender or supplier may give you. Watch hand movements, facial expressions, and changes in posture. You may be far more aware of other people's body language than they are. For example, the pupils of a person's eyes may expand when that person is pleased by or interested in something you have said. You will be aware of this; the other person will not.

## Your Personal Style

People may not remember your words or your accomplishments, but they rarely forget your style. With this in mind, be true to your own perception of yourself. Do nothing that doesn't "feel right." In other words, be yourself.

# 4

# The Laws of Entrepreneurship

## SILVER'S FIRST LAW OF ENTREPRENEURSHIP

The creation of wealth by entrepreneurial means is the result of three interrelated components:

1. The size of the problem that the entrepreneur has formulated
2. The elegance of the entrepreneur's solution to that problem—that is, the uniqueness and appropriateness of the product or the non-duplicability of the marketing system
3. The quality and competence of the entrepreneurial team

This law might also be called Silver's first law of venture capital. Whichever term you choose to use, the law is expressed in the following equation:

$$V = P \times S \times E$$

where
  $V$ = Valuation, or wealth
  $P$ = Size of the problem
  $S$ = Elegance of the solution
  $E$ = Excellence of the entrepreneurial team

The greater the values one can achieve for $P$, $S$, and $E$, the greater will be the valuation of the entrepreneurial company and the wealth of its founder and early investors. The factors $P$, $S$, and $E$ are interrelated. If all of them are large, the valuation will be very large. But if just one of them has a zero value, the venture will be worthless and the capital invested in it will be lost. Let's relate this simple but fundamental equation to three imaginary entrepreneurs who lived at the dawn of civilization:

Far back among the mists of time, a family prepared a feast for some important visitors from another tribe. In doing so, they created productivity, employment, and innovation.

The family hunted and killed many birds, harvested vegetables, and picked fruit and coconuts to feed their guests. They persuaded a friend to cut down a tree and build them a table and benches for the guests' comfort. They asked others to clear an area from the jungle in which the feast could be held. Still others were asked to cook, serve, and clear away the meal. All told, a dozen people worked on the feast, and the family promised each of them a reward when the feast was over.

The feast was lavish and beautifully prepared. It tasted better than any meal the visitors had ever eaten. They promised to reciprocate, and a week later they sent the host family a fine goat as a thank-you present. The family gave goat's milk to all of the people who had helped them prepare the feast. The workers were so pleased with the way the law of reciprocity worked that they eagerly volunteered to help prepare another feast, and another, and another.

As the feast business flourished and was transformed into a large-scale restaurant operation, however, some of the workers grew bored with performing the same tasks day after day. One of them, the table maker, left the first entrepreneur's team and built himself a floating table, which he called a boat. He planned to purchase food from the feast-giver, load it into his boat, transport it to nearby islands, and sell it to the tribes who lived there. The family of restaurant owners saw this enterprise as a second source of revenue, so they invested in the food exporting business.

Life is random, however, and rewards are uncertain. When the exporter arrived on the nearby island with his cargo of food, the tribe welcomed him with cries of joy and offered him a thousand coconuts as his reward. But it was not the food that they wanted, for they had plenty of that; it was his boat.

They explained to him that their island was heavily populated, a situation that had created a tremendous waste-removal problem. If the visitor would make boats for them, however, they would easily be able to cart their waste away.

Like many an entrepreneur in the centuries to follow, this food exporter found that he had to make a major change in his plans. There was no food shortage problem for him to solve, so he had to give up the export business. There was, however, a serious need for boats. Because all good entrepreneurs are flexible, the food exporter quickly transformed himself into a boat manufacturer. Also, this entrepreneur had learned management skills by working for the restaurateur, which gave the E (entrepreneurial team) factor of his boat-making enterprise a high value. He had, in other words, all three components of the formula: a large problem, a good solution, and an excellent entrepreneurial team—himself and the workers he trained.

One of the boat maker's cleverest workers achieved a high-technology breakthrough: he invented the wheel. Initially, however, he had a very large S (solution) for which he had to find a P (problem)—or, preferably, several P's. Eventually he, too, decided to use his invention to solve the widespread problem of waste removal. To that end he and his family began to produce wheelbarrows, which could be used to cart the waste to the shore where the second entrepreneur's boats waited. After firmly establishing his wheelbarrow business, he took advantage of many other entrepreneurial opportunities by setting up a waste-hauling enterprise, a wheel-manufacturing business, and dozens of other operations that relied on the wheel.

As the years passed, many other entrepreneurships were spun off from the original three. The circle of problem solving kept widening to include more and more solutions and receivers of those solutions. Service organizations were established, and the manufacture of components became an important industry. The tribal people came to understand that their profits would exceed their costs by a significant margin as long as three circumstances prevailed:

1. The solutions had to solve large problems for the receivers.
2. The solutions had to be unique or presented in a unique, nonduplicable manner.
3. The law of reciprocity had to be obeyed to the letter.

Many inventor-entrepreneurs (like the one who invented the wheel) develop elegant solutions first and then find suitable problems for them. Note that the formulation of a problem is crucial, however, for no matter how elegant and unique the solution may be, it is of little value—or *no* value—if it is not needed to solve a serious problem. Contrary to Benjamin Franklin's claim, people will not beat a path to your door if you develop a better mousetrap, for that is a solution which lacks a serious problem.

Multiple revenue sources exist for each of the three entrepreneurial companies in the story. Competent entrepreneurs are capable of multiplying their $V$ (wealth) by introducing new $S$s and offering them to the established receivers via unique methods. For example, the family of restaurateurs could open additional restaurants on nearby islands, sell franchises to tribes on faraway islands, package their delicacies for sale at boat docks, launch a gourmet magazine, and publish their recipes. The boat manufacturer could start a rent-a-boat business or operate boats under contract for islands that prefer to have their transport needs managed by someone more experienced than themselves. The wheelbarrow manufacturer could establish a wheelbarrow rental agency, operate a garbage removal business under contract for tribes who prefer that service, and exploit his wheel as a component part of other products.

There is a rule of thumb that for every job created by an entrepreneurial company one additional job is created in the community to service the employee and his or her family. These jobs are filled by teachers, beauticians, clerks, service station attendants, and the like.

Note the myriad services for which these first three entrepreneurs created a need. The restaurant entrepreneurs created a need for laundry, linen supply, printing of menus, graphic art for signs and menus, garbage removal, fresh flowers for their tables, furniture, music for their well-known ambience, uniforms for the waiters and waitresses, and advertising and public relations to inform receivers about their service. With further expansion, the first entrepreneurs will require day-care services for their employees' children, lawyers to draft franchising agreements, and a marketing team to sell their delicacies at boat docks and to sell franchises to faraway tribes.

The services created by the second entrepreneur, the boat maker, include leasing consultants, travel agents to schedule trips for his sales personnel, bankers to open letters of credit, and facilities management consultants to assist the entrepreneur in pricing and operating his transportation management services to other islands.

The third entrepreneur, the inventor, needs assistance in industrial design because his wheels, which are made of coconuts, have a tendency to crack when a heavy load is carted in the wheelbarrow. He also needs engineers, financial consultants, and management consultants. Inventor-entrepreneurs seem to require the greatest number of service professionals to fill the gaps in their knowledge.

By contrast, job-creating ability of nonentrepreneurial companies is very small, and in many instances negative. In fact, between 1970 and 1980, the thousand largest companies in the United States reduced their number of employees by three million. During the same decade, approximately twenty million new jobs were created by companies five years of age or under.

Entrepreneurs, in other words, generate not only wealth but also jobs, many of which are in the community at large rather than inside the company headquarters. As new businesses are established, they create a need for myriad service employees in the adjacent area: accountants, lawyers, advertising and marketing people, maintenance crews, teachers, and health care personnel.

Another development often occurs as entrepreneurial companies are established: local citizens receive an opportunity to invest in them. In many instances, however, these people do not fully understand the first law of entrepreneurship—$V = P \times S \times E$—and as a result, they lose their investment. They may mistakenly believe, for example, that all three factors in the formula have a high value when one of them actually has no value at all.

Over the next few years, however, as people learn more about venture capital investing, losses of this kind will decline rapidly. Several major brokerage firms have offered opportunities for the $5,000 investor to participate in venture capital funds managed by experienced investors. More such funds will be created in the future, but the securities laws will have to be modified before venture capital investment can become as popular as commodities, options, and puts and calls. State laws that make it difficult or impossible for local citizens to invest in entrepreneurial companies will also have to be modified in order for states to attract entrepreneurs to launch businesses within their borders. The states with the most stringent "blue sky" laws (those laws that restrict the sale of securities of entrepreneurial companies to local, unsophisticated investors) generally have the fewest entrepreneurial success stories to boast about.

## Putting the Formula to Work

The formula $V = P \times S \times E$ is the fundamental law of the entrepreneurial process. It explains why some new enterprises succeed and others fail. Assume for example that the maximum value for $P$, $S$, and $E$ is 3 and that their minimum value is 0. Then the greatest venture capital or entrepreneurial opportunity would have an initial score of 27 ($V = 3 \times 3 \times 3$). On the other hand, the worst venture capital or entrepreneurial opportunity would have an initial score of 0, *but* that zero could be arrived at in many ways: $1 \times 1 \times 0 = 0$; $0 \times 2 \times 3 = 0$; $3 \times 0 \times 3 = 0$; and so forth. In between these two extreme scores are the majority of entrepreneurial opportunities. The $3 \times 3 \times 3$ situations are extremely rare, although they have occurred perhaps on fifty to seventy-five occasions in the last twenty-five years. I described some of them in *Entrepreneurial Megabucks: The 100 Greatest Entrepreneurs of the Last Twenty-Five Years* (New York: Wiley, 1985). The *V* factors of these 100 companies average approximately $1 billion on an average initial capital of $150,000, and each of these businesses created 40,000 new jobs on average.

Exhibit 4.1 shows ten of the highest-*V* entrepreneurial companies, their initial capital, their 1985 valuations, and their rates of return.

A close examination of the *P*, *S*, and *E* of those ten companies will show you why they have achieved such high valuations: the value of all three factors in the formula was extremely high for each company.

To further demonstrate the utility of the first law of entrepreneurship, let's look at some of the greatest entrepreneurial failures of recent memory and see which of the factors—*P*, *S*, or *E*—was missing (Exhibit 4.2).

Bear in mind that some fairly experienced venture capital investors perceived these companies as having positive values in their *P*, *S*, and *E* accounts, when in fact at least one of the factors was worth zero in each company listed in Exhibit 4.2.

In the case of DeLorean Motor Company it is generally believed that *all* of the factors had either zero or almost zero values.

Let's examine those factors one at a time. First of all, the problem DeLorean formulated—a need for expensive sports cars—was nonexistent. Porsche, Jaguar, Nissan, and other manufacturers were already battling fiercely for the attention of the $25,000-and-up car buyer, and there was simply no need for another manufacturer to enter the field. In this instance, then, *P* equaled zero.

As for the second factor, DeLorean provided a solution that was not unique, and he proceeded to market that solution in a way that was easily duplicable. Thus *S* also equaled zero.

The *E* factor—the entrepreneurial team—did appear to have positive value during the start-up phase of the company. John Z. DeLorean, by all measures, was a corporate achiever with a distinguished track record at General Motors. With his departure from GM and the publication of his book, *On a Clear Day You Can See General Motors*, it appeared that DeLorean was making the traditional passage from dissatisfied, bored manager to driven, energetic, self-fulfilled entrepreneur. The rapid demise of his automobile company and the steps that he took to save it have since raised serious questions about DeLorean's competence, but in the early days, the *E* factor must have looked very attractive. Nonetheless, even if his entrepreneurial team deserved a 3, this value, when multiplied by the two zeroes in the *P* and *S* accounts, would have resulted in a clear and resounding zero.

*Exhibit 4.1. Ten of the Greatest Vs of the Last Forty Years*

| Name of Company | Founded | Description of Business | Capital | 1985 V ($ millions) | Return on Investment |
|---|---|---|---|---|---|
| 1. Wal-Mart Stores, Inc. | 1962 | Discount stores | Pers. sav. | $3,400 | Infinite |
| 2. Wang Laboratories | 1955 | Minicomputers | Pers. sav. | 4,100 | Infinite |
| 3. McDonald's Corp. | 1961 | Fast food | Pers. sav. | 4,200 | Infinite |
| 4. Intel Corp. | 1968 | Semiconductors | $2 million | 2,000 | 100 times |
| 5. Honda Motor Co. | 1948 | Mopeds, cars | Pers. sav. | 4,400 | Infinite |
| 6. Sony Corp. | 1946 | Pocket electronics | Pers. sav. | 3,500 | Infinite |
| 7. Hospital Corp. of America | 1968 | Hospital chain | Pers. sav. | 3,400 | Infinite |
| 8. Electronic Data Systems | 1962 | Facilities mgmt. | $20,000 | 2,500 | 1,000,000 times |
| 9. Holiday Inns of America | 1952 | Motel chain | Pers. sav. | 3,700 | Infinite |
| 10. Rolm Corp. | 1969 | Telephone systems | $1.2 million | 1,500 | 125 times |

*Exhibit 4.2. Large Entrepreneurial Failures of the Last Ten Years*

| Name of Company | Date Founded | Type of Business | Wasted ($000) | Primary Investors |
|---|---|---|---|---|
| 1. DeLorean Motor Co. | 1978 | Expensive cars | 134,000 | R&D LP |
| 2. U.S. Football League | 1982 | Sports league | 120,000 | Private investors |
| 3. Ibis Corp. | 1983 | Minicomputers | 85,000 | Venture capital |
| 4. Air Florida Corp. | 1979 | Regional airline | 75,000 | Venture capital |
| 5. Z-Tel | 1983 | Telephone equipment | 56,000[a] | Venture capital |
| 6. Florida Data Corp. | 1982 | Minicomputer | 35,000 | Venture capital |
| 7. Osborne Computer Corp. | 1982 | Portable computer | 25,000 | Venture capital |
| 8. Mindset Corp. | 1983 | Personal computer | 18,500 | Venture capital |
| 9. Gavilan Computer | 1983 | Lap-top computer | 15,000 | Venture capital |
| 10. Otrona Corp. | 1983 | Portable computer | 15,000 | Venture capital |

[a] $17 million recently raised to emerge from Chapter XI.

The DeLorean example vividly illustrates the importance of formulating a very large $P$, developing a unique $S$—either protected by patents or conveyed to the market in an innovative manner—and assembling an entrepreneurial team that includes one or more corporate achievers.

Each of these three factors—problem, solution, and entrepreneurial team—is vital to the success of the enterprise. In fact, the demise of many businesses, both small and large, is a direct result of the neglect of one or more of the factors. To illustrate this, let's talk about each factor as it could be applied to specific enterprises.

## Problem Formulation

Think for a moment of the many stores and small service organizations that open in your community and close before the end of their first full year of operation. These quick failures are often the result of faulty problem formulation: many people go into business in order to solve a problem *for themselves,* whereas the successful entrepreneur goes into business to solve problems *for others.*

The person who loves clothing may long to quit her job and open a clothing shop. But she spends no time at all thinking about the ways in which she can solve problems for her potential customers. All she thinks about is whether the shop will serve as a solution to her own problems— boredom in her old job, lack of financial independence, the need to work in a field that doesn't interest her, the difficulty of coping with the whims of her current boss, to name a few.

On the other side of town, a person who loves books decides to open a bookstore—again, to solve his own problems, one of which is the torture of a long commute to his old job. To avoid the commute, he establishes the store close to his home, and to satisfy his love of books, he stocks the shop with the works of his favorite authors.

Both of these merchants are doomed to failure before they even begin. They are providing gifts to themselves, not to others; they have neglected to formulate $P$ with the necessary care and thought.

Not all new entrepreneurs make this mistake, of course. The good ones spend plenty of time and energy formulating the problem they wish to solve *for others.*

There may exist in your community a number of small businesses that have become successful. You can be sure there is an entrepreneur behind them. Notice the high level of service to the customer, an accurate measure of the entrepreneur's decision to solve other people's problems. Notice also the excitement of the store or restaurant, the hustle and bustle of the employees, the chatter of the customers as they discuss the product.

Robert F. Sikora went into business for others—the mark of a true entrepreneur. When he opened Bobby McGee's Conglomeration, Inc., a restaurant/discotheque in Scottsdale, Arizona, he had the waiters and waitresses dress up like comic book characters because he believed that "normal people should have as much fun at night as cowboys." (Sikora had previously opened Mr. Lucky's, a popular country-and-western nightclub in Phoenix, where I entered one night in a suit and tie, only to have the tie cut in half by the doorman.) There are now 21 Bobby McGee restaurants, and on some weekend nights, 300 people wait in line to get in.

Successful entrepreneurs like Sikora attend very carefully to the formulation of the problem. Prior to launching a new enterprise, the competent entrepreneurs ask themselves not only *who* needs their product but also *where* these people can be found. In other words, they carefully examine all of the available selling sites and choose the one that is most easily accessible to potential customers.

A cookie store, for example, is unlikely to do well on the suburban street near your home. That location might be convenient for you, but it will not pull in the hundreds of people who feel the need of a midmorning snack. You would do best to set up shop in an enclosed mall, where the aroma of vanilla will attract crowds of passersby who need a bite to carry them through another two hours of shopping. Flower shops also succeed where there is plenty of foot traffic. The sight and smell of flowers makes people want to take some beauty home with them.

When successful entrepreneurs set out to formulate the *P* factor, they also take several other things into consideration. One important factor is the *homogeneity of the receivers:* Will the product have to be customized or will one standard item be suitable to all? Another consideration is the *receivers' attitude toward the problem:* Do they realize they have a problem or have they grown accustomed to living with it? And a third factor is *the value that the receivers will place on your solution:* How much will they be willing to pay for the product or service? The entrepreneur can answer this last question by conducting market research and organizing focus groups.

Problem formulation, then, is a creative but time-consuming initial step in the entrepreneurial process. Many small business persons fail to devote sufficient time, energy, and thought to it because they are too eager to give *themselves* a gift; their primary goal is to "leave the jerk I work for and go into business for myself."

### Finding the Solution

The *S* factor—the solution to the problem—is poorly conceived just as frequently. Business owners often seem to forget that a solution alone will not guarantee success, no matter how large its opportunity. The innovation must be marketed in a unique and nonduplicable way. Financial institutions, both large and small, often make the mistake of neglecting the marketing methods. They fall all over themselves offering new services, but most of them fail to train their employees to explain the services to the receivers. They may also give inadequate instructions in its use and offer too little after-sale support.

Commercial banks provide a good example of this tendency to neglect the planning of the S factor. Many of these banks reacted to Merrill Lynch's innovative cash management account (CMA) with virtually identical products of their own, but they met with relatively little success. They marketed IRA accounts on a price basis only, to attract cash into their banks, without describing the beneficial features of IRAs, such as purchasing common stocks, art, or artifacts. Investment banks have introduced dozens of products into the market over the last ten years: commodities, options, puts and calls, certificates of deposit, repos, Ginnie Maes, Fannie Maes, Sallie Maes, and so on. The account executives have been hard pressed to learn the features of one product before the next one is introduced by a senior management team that is long on funding innovation but short on devoting thought and time to customer service or after-sale support.

When I dived into the entrepreneurial waters several years ago with a new retail computer chain in southern California, it was with the thought that if my sales and service personnel could provide their customers with better service and after-sale support, we would obtain a greater market share. Like financial institutions, computer manufacturers introduce new products two or three times a year, and advertise them heavily to create market awareness. They expect the retail computer chains to buy the new products on thirty-day terms, learn their features, integrate them with appropriate software and peripheral equipment, advertise their availability, train and instruct the customer, and then wait forty-five to sixty days to receive payment, which is frequently delayed until several service calls are made. Naturally, the problem-solving methods of many computer manufacturers have been less than satisfactory. Thus the retail chains that have carefully selected their vendors and built customer loyalty and allegiance with a well-trained service organization have become successful. Frequently *how* one gives the gift is more important than the gift itself.

As you begin to formulate the S factor for your enterprise, you should ask yourself this question: What audience do I want to address? It is important to answer this question thoughtfully, because as a small-business person you must *like* the individuals to whom you provide solutions.

People often ask me this question: "How do I decide which business I should go into?" I answer by asking two questions of my own:

1. What group of people would you most enjoy solving a problem for?
2. If you could walk across a stage five years from now and receive the applause of two hundred people, which group of people would you most like to have applauding you?

When you become an entrepreneur, it is crucial for you to like your receivers. After all is said and done, they are your primary audience. For example, my audience is the universe of entrepreneurs. If they perceive the value of my books as greater than I do, then I will receive their applause.

If you like to be in the presence of a certain group of people, you will find it all the sweeter to solve a problem for them. The opposite is unfortunately true as well. For example, if commercial bank managers *liked* their depositors, they wouldn't make them wait in line for thirty minutes to withdraw their money. Undoubtedly the first bankers, the entrepreneurs of banking, liked their customers. However, with the growth in size of banks, the redirection of bank personnel and capital toward products and away from services, the receiver of banking services can honestly say, "I do not value my bank's services very highly." Is it any wonder that the U.S. commercial banking industry is far less profitable today than it once was?

Spend time right now thinking about which group of people you want to help and then think of the various things you could do to solve problems for that audience. If you like children, for example, you can select from among numerous entrepreneurial opportunities. Children need solutions to many different problems: low reading scores, the danger of exposure to drugs and alcohol, the increase in teenage suicide. Can you develop solutions to problems like these and offer them to an audience of children?

If you like children and sports, keep this entrepreneurial idea in mind: Lacrosse is very popular with boys, but there is no organization akin to baseball's Little League to accelerate its growth and expansion.

An equally large number of opportunities exists for those who would like to help older people cope with problems. Never before have so many people in America been over sixty-five years of age. In fact, the fastest growing segment of the population is over eighty. If the hands that you want to hear applauding you as you walk across the stage five years from now are the hands of senior citizens, you will find some very large problem-solving opportunities in this marketplace.

Some people, especially inventors, begin with an *S* and then seek a group of receivers who need that solution. This can be an easy search, as it was for the entrepreneur who invented the wheel, or a long and difficult one. Many entrepreneur-inventors have, in fact, faltered at this stage. Chester Carlson, for example, invented Xerography—a fine solution—but failed to recognize the enormous audience for it. Carlson believed the process would be useful to patent lawyers such as himself who had to make very accurate photocopies of patents. It was left to others to see the widespread problem that photocopying could solve.

Inventor-entrepreneurs frequently fail to achieve great wealth because the gifts they have to offer are of relatively little value to the particular receivers they have in mind. To avoid this pitfall, do some homework to find those receivers who have the greatest need for your invention.

## The Entrepreneurial Team

Assume for a moment that several experienced venture capitalists, prior to making an investment, are told, "Here is your start-up company, and here are three values: 1.5, 1.5, and 3. Now assign each of those three numbers to the factors *P*, *S*, and *E* in any manner you choose." How do you think those knowledgeable venture capitalists would proceed? Chances are there would be no hesitation and no argument among them. They would pin the 3 on the *E* factor. Because they are experienced in the entrepreneurial field, these investors understand that the enterprise must be placed in the hands of people who have been members of entrepreneurial teams in the past. They also know that a competent corporate achiever is frequently sufficient to pull a company out of difficulty, especially if the entrepreneurial team is backed by an experienced board of directors who have a stake in the company.

Start-up entrepreneurs, on the other hand, frequently fail because of a lack of experience and know-how—in other words, because they give too little consideration to the critical *E* factor. In many instances they appear to be so blissfully unaware of the dangers of venturing into the business world with an incompetent or naive management that they fail even to seek training or to enlist the aid of consultants in those areas in which they are untrained—typically, marketing and finance.

To some extent the Small Business Administration (SBA) stands at fault here. As I mentioned in Chapter 3, the SBA has given financial assistance to many beginning entrepreneurs, which is generally a good thing. However, it has tended to hand out loans and to guarantee SBICs and MESBICs without regard for the amount, or lack, of experience of the potential business owner. As a result, a large proportion of SBA borrowers have gone into businesses that subsequently failed. In fact, more SBIC and MESBIC borrowers have failed than have succeeded. The SBA program has been scaled back in recent years, partly because its critics claim that it has helped place inadequately trained business-people in the marketplace. Without the SBA, there might be more emphasis on learning how to become a competent manager before leaping into business head first.

If you are a wise entrepreneur, then, you will make use of available consultants and training courses before entering the business world. You will also assemble a management team composed of men and women who have demonstrated their ability to introduce new products, get those products to the market on schedule, build a sales and service team, and meet or beat a budget. You can entice these men and women into your company with a material equity incentive, an opportunity to run their own show, and the lure of the "chase"—the chance to build a winning enterprise.

Another avenue of opportunity is open to the would-be entrepreneur who has less than a treasure trove of management experience, and that is the franchise. One of the most compelling arguments for franchising is that the purchasers of franchises (franchisees) remain in business five years longer ninety percent of the time than do other small-business persons, who fail within the first five years ninety percent of the time.

By looking again at our formula, we can see why franchisees have a more successful track record. Unlike the independent business owner, who is responsible for all three factors in the formula, the franchisee has most of the burden taken off his or her shoulders right from the beginning. In a franchise operation, the franchisor has already formulated $P$ and developed $S$, relieving the franchisee of this responsibility. As for the $E$ factor, the beginner still has a great deal to learn, but he or she will not have to do so alone. The franchisor will provide budgets and financial statements of other franchisees, advertisements that worked in other communities, and a manual of operations that tells what each employee should be doing every moment of the day or night. Franchisees can call for assistance, meet with other franchisees at training seminars, go to the home office for answers to questions, and enlist the franchisor's aid in selling the franchise should they wish to retire. Franchisees pay a substantial up-front fee to purchase proven franchises, or a small up-front fee for the unproven ones. The fee separates the amateurs who want to "go into business for themselves" from the givers, who would like to serve the audience that the particular franchisor has selected.

## SILVER'S SECOND LAW: THE LAW OF THE BIG P

*The valuation of a company is equal to the size of the problem addressed and is often achieved before the solution to that problem is delivered.*

The law of the big *P* helps to explain the prices of certain publicly held stocks, which are unjustified by earnings. It also explains, perhaps, why our stock market is vibrant while stocks languish in countries that lack the optimism of the U.S. stock-buying public.

Just as Americans seem to love movies that have exciting chase scenes, so too do they love new publicly held companies that set out to chase disease, hunger, and illness with weapons such as interferon, monoclonal antibodies, and other breakthroughs in medical technology. One such company is Cetus Corporation, which fights the big *P* of hunger by genetically engineering seeds that will affix to the sandy soil of the Sudan. This company has a market value in excess of $1 billion, with the prospect for earnings many years off into the future. Another company, Genentech, armed with gene-splicing and recombinant DNA skills, chases diabetes, cancer, hoof-and-mouth disease, and dwarfism. Its market value exceeds $1.2 billion, and significant earnings are very far in the future—a measure of how successfully *S* is being conveyed by *E*.

Cetus, Genentech, and other biotechnology companies are chasing big *P*'s with elegant *S*'s and experienced *E*'s. They are able to go to the public market and to R&D limited partnerships for bales of capital because the typical investor loves a good chase. Large pharmaceutical manufacturers are courting the big-*P* companies as well, in hope of winning marketing licenses to the breakthrough *S*'s.

Because of high investor interest in companies of this sort, the entrepreneur can often achieve financial success during the start-up period, as the law of the big *P* states. This provides a strong argument in favor of establishing a company whose goal is to solve a very big *P*.

Keep in mind, however, that big-*P* companies, once they begin to achieve earnings, frequently drop in price. Analysts begin to scrutinize their earnings and financial ratios, and a price-earnings ratio is assigned to their industry. As earnings arrive, so does the solution (*S*). And once the solution begins to be delivered, big *P* no longer exists. Wise entrepreneurs sell some of their position before this happens.

A thorough understanding of the law of the big *P* is vital on a personal as well as an economic level. Entrepreneurship is an arduous process that requires at least five years of great personal sacrifice—eighty-hour work weeks, a severely reduced social life, sometimes the endangerment of close relationships or even a marriage. It seems foolish to risk all of this in order to establish a small-$P$ company producing a me-too commodity that no one really needs. Why not make the sacrifice worthwhile by addressing one of the many large social or medical problems that exist in the world today? The personal rewards you will gain—from reducing the risk of heart attacks, for example, or from improving the lives of old people—will make your hard work worthwhile. Big dreams, after all, are the stuff of which American heroes are made.

## SILVER'S THIRD LAW: RISK AVERSION

*It is necessary to assemble a team of corporate achievers to manage other aspects of the company so as to leave the entrepreneur free to handle research and development and manufacturing start-up.*

If you are a competent entrepreneur, you will identify all risks associated with each step you are about to take. Then you will contemplate several "what if" scenarios and determine what your own response will be in case each of those scenarios develops.

One of the most successful venture capital investors in the United States, Timothy A. G. Hay, president of Security Pacific Capital Corporation, calls this "downside planning"—being prepared for the worst that could possibly happen. "The most competent entrepreneurs always hear footsteps coming up behind them," Hay says. "They are continually planning how they will deal with the footsteps, how they will avert risk."

To better understand risk aversion, think in terms of the five stages in the life of a new company:

1. Research and development
2. Manufacturing start-up
3. Marketing
4. Management
5. Growth

Competent entrepreneurs typically assume risk at the research and development and the manufacturing stages of the launch, but they hand off the risks of the other three stages to others. Let us understand the five stages in the life of a new company and then examine how the better entrepreneurs avoid risk.

### Research and Development

Think of research as problem formulation, and development as creating the solution. Depending on the nature of the problem—industrial, social, recreational, or medical—the formulation may require weeks, months, or years. It will mean learning how many people have the problem, finding out if the receivers are homogeneous, determining if they realize they have a problem, and estimating the price they would pay for an effective solution. Problem formulation is the most important step in entrepreneurship, and it is ongoing throughout the life of the new company. Without a continuous emphasis on understanding the receivers and their needs, your solutions may eventually fail to satisfy.

Creating the solution also can require weeks, months, or years, depending on the nature of the solution and its delivery method. In high-technology, capital equipment, and consumer product companies, the uniqueness of the solution is of critical importance, and several years of product design, development, and testing are required. Remember that the first wheelbarrow could not be produced until the wheel was invented. Similarly, several years of product design, development, and testing may be necessary before your product can be offered to the public. In companies of this sort, then, you as the entrepreneur must assume risk in the R&D phase.

Other kinds of companies, however, may pose less risk for the entrepreneur. In facilities management, franchising, and newsletter-seminar packaging, for example, a solution can often be designed and developed reasonably quickly, often on the customer's facilities and with the customer's capital and assets.

In establishing a company of any kind, however, you will have to assume some risk during the R&D phase. The amount of risk you face will depend in large part on the type of company you choose to establish.

In most kinds of companies, you should be able to begin the R&D phase while still working at your old job. Exhausting as this may turn out to be, it ensures that nothing will be at risk except time; you will not be risking the loss of your livelihood as well. Also keep in mind that if the *P* is sufficiently large, potential customers and others can be persuaded to finance the research-and-development stage. You can leverage a big *P*. Thus you will need to assume only part of the R&D risk.

## Manufacturing

At the manufacturing stage, the emphasis shifts to producing a commodity that the receivers need and will value highly. Here all of the responsibility for risk falls on the shoulders of the entrepreneur—you. At this point you must test, debug, and retest your product, put it into the hands of potential consumers for more testing, and then package it effectively.

During this stage, your new company is likely to run a cash flow deficit, which must be funded by leveraging customers, suppliers, employees (by having them work overtime), family, friends, lenders, and investors. As time passes, the amount of risk you face will be more closely related to the value of your product: if the receivers consistently value your company's solutions more highly than you do, most of the company's continuing need for capital will be financed up front by customers, and the amount of risk you as the entrepreneur must bear will be reduced.

## Marketing

Once you move into the marketing phase, your company will begin to grow rapidly and will incur large cash flow deficits. At this point, however, you will have become risk averse and hired managers to oversee many of its functions and attracted an experienced board of directors to advise the managers. Also at this phase, various segments of the company will be subdivided in order to ensure appropriate attention to detail by those managers. The marketing area, for example, will be subdivided into sales, advertising, public relations, telemarketing, after-sale support, customer service, and administrative support. Production, finance, and the other critical functional areas will go through a similar stratification. The cash flow deficit is now reduced via intensive leveraging of all interested parties and, if that is inadequate, by selling equity interests to venture capitalists. Thus you as the entrepreneur will now bear less risk.

## Management

Your new company has demonstrated that its solution satisfies the needs of many receivers. The enterprise is profitable and growing rapidly. By now you have stepped aside, and the managers are making most of the day-to-day operating decisions. At this stage, they are beginning to consider various options: merger into a similar or complementary company, an initial public offering to diversify the entrepreneurial team's wealth into other assets and (a not mutually exclusive option) raise ancillary capital to develop additional and complementary products—or, as they are generally called, "models." Depending on a number of factors, many of which have to do with the management abilities of the members of $E$ and whether or not they enjoy working together, your company will either merge into a larger company at this point or go public and maintain a unique identity.

## Growth

At the growth stage, your new company usually has all of its functional areas filled by experienced managers, and its products have solved long ago the problems they were designed for. The problems, in fact, may have been long forgotten, and by now the public may mention your solution reverently, as in "Do you remember what life was like before Federal Express?" If so, you will indeed have become a giver, and your gifts will have become basic components of daily life.

It is during the growth stage, however, that many companies lose their most important managers. If the value of their stock options provides these key people with enough capital, they often decide to explore the entrepreneurial waters for themselves. If too many of your company's most energetic and innovative employees leave to do other things, your company's solutions will begin to lose their value, and the sales growth pattern will start to flatten.

As I said earlier, you, the entrepreneur, generally will be materially at risk in only two of these five stages in the growth of a new company: R&D and manufacturing start-up. If you hire an experienced corporate achiever to run the operation, the risks associated with the other stages will be assumed by the management team you have assembled.

Most economists are incorrect in their assessment of entrepreneurs as gun-slinging risk takers who hit the beach firing in every direction, then run toward a target that falls down. Competent entrepreneurs are careful planners who consider all of the possible "what-ifs," then plan for the worst that can happen. Successful entrepreneurs contemplate a worst-case scenario for each major step they take and plan an escape route in the event the worst happens. All the while they maintain and project an optimistic, can-do attitude in order to persuade customers, vendors, employers, lenders, and investors that the most optimistic scenario will occur and that they are a vital part of the dream. This kind of optimism is vital to the success of the entrepreneurial process. The image of a bold, swashbuckling entrepreneur must be presented to the public from time to time, but the winning entrepreneurial formula is based on careful planning and systematic risk aversion.

# 5

## Generic Entrepreneurial Opportunities

You want to be an entrepreneur and you have what it takes: heart, patience, drive, an understanding of leverage, an ability to cooperate, and courage. You have become dissatisfied with your current job, and you have the energy to launch and build your own company. Finally, you have read some books about being an entrepreneur, attended seminars on the subject, and either worked for or been given advice by a successful entrepreneur. You now understand the basic laws that were discussed in the preceding chapter and that govern the entrepreneurial process. Now it is time to examine the opportunities from which you may choose.

Later in this book, we will discuss some very specific entrepreneurial opportunities. For now, however, we are going to look at the broad generic areas in which these opportunities can be found. It is here that you will decide what kind of entrepreneur you wish to be. The five generic entrepreneurial opportunities (GEOs) are as follows:

- Big problems
- Medium-sized problems
- Niche problems

- Elegant solutions
- Leveraged buy-outs

Let's examine these GEOs individually to see what sort of problem solving each of them involves.

## Big Problems

If you become a big-problem entrepreneur, you will turn your energy toward solving one of society's major difficulties, a problem of heroic proportions that affects millions of people. Here are some big problems in need of solutions:

- Hunger
- Crime
- Drug abuse
- Terrorism

Big-problem entrepreneurs address issues that are national or even international in scope. They select enormous problems and they build large entrepreneurial organizations to try to solve them. The moral imperative of the big-problem entrepreneur is to leave a very large mark on society. These people see themselves and their mission in heroic terms.

## Medium-sized Problems

A medium-sized problem affects a smaller number of people—say, half a million—and does not have the life-or-death drama of the big-problem GEO. Medium-sized problems include:

- High cost of prisons
- Computer obsolescence
- Traffic jams in cities
- High cost of college

Medium-sized problems attract entrepreneurs who wish to solve statewide or regional problems. They see the rise of crime in their state as a problem. They are appalled by local transportation problems. They urgently seek to ease the overcrowding in local prisons, schools, or nursing homes. They love their region and wish to improve it in a certain way. These entrepreneurs seize the chance to make an important contribution to the people in their city, state, or region. Frequently their companies expand nationally, but their initial intent is to be a regional problem solver.

## Niche Problems

Niche problems are less than medium-sized and last for only a brief time, until an item that was once very costly can be produced for a medium price, or until a once inexpensive item can be produced in a higher quality and at a higher price. Here are some niche problems:

- The lack of convenient videocassette dispensing machines
- The need for reasonably priced, effective oil additives

Niche-problem entrepreneurs are the most plentiful. They usually have less to lose if their company fails to grow and develop. These entrepreneurs did not shoot too high and thus will not fall too far. The popular entrepreneurial magazines are peppered with stories about niche-market entrepreneurs—vertical market software companies, used-car rental agencies, videocassette distribution centers, computer software stores, home fitness equipment manufacturers, and new restaurant concepts.

## Elegant Solutions

Elegant solutions are produced at great expense but without thought as to who—if anyone—needs them. This GEO is most often the choice of the inventor-entrepreneur. Recent examples of elegant solutions in search of problems include:

- Feminine deodorant spray
- Lettuce cigarettes
- Jojoba oil
- Wind power

An elegant-solutions entrepreneur is usually an inventive person who has discovered a means of making something that is unique and that has several different applications. If you fall into this category, you'll want to select an appropriate application at the outset by very careful problem formulation.

## Leveraged Buy-Outs

For entrepreneurs who do not wish to address one of society's problems and who have not invented an elegant solution to a problem, but who earnestly wish to own and operate their own company, there is the leveraged buy-out (LBO). In this GEO the entrepreneur raises the capital necessary to buy an existing company by borrowing on its assets and repaying the debt out of cash flow or the sale of assets. Numerous entrepreneurs have acquired small companies through the LBO route and have built them into major enterprises. Some of the better known LBO entrepreneurs and their companies are:

- Royal Little, Textron Corporation
- Charles Bluhdorn, Gulf + Western Corporation
- Henry E. Singleton, Teledyne, Inc.
- William Farley, Farley Industries, Inc.
- William Y. Tauscher, FoxMeyer Corporation

Which of these GEOs is best for you? The answer depends on several conditions. First, who will make up the audience for which you wish to solve problems and from which you want to receive applause? If you enjoy solving teenagers' problems, for example, you can choose from among an unusually large number of unaddressed problems, including eating disorders, suicide, stress, stepparenting issues, and substance abuse.

Many opportunities have arisen in the health-care delivery field since that marketplace began to change from a seller's to a buyer's market. Medical costs must be lowered, without a diminution in quality, in order for hospitals, physicians, and clinics to remain viable. If you enjoy solving problems for physicians, and if you are computer literate, you might choose juxtaposing efficient information systems onto the health-care delivery market. This field will present dozens of entrepreneurial opportunities through the end of the twentieth century.

Which of these GEOs is best for you? To determine the answer to that important question, examine each GEO again to determine whether or not it is suitable to you, given your knowledge, skills, experience, and character.

For example, if you have a wide knowledge of pharmaceuticals and their use in treating disease, you may decide to examine one of the big-problem GEOs such as the need for a method of treating diabetes or cancer. If you do *not* have excellent financial skills, you will undoubtedly see that the LBO is not for you. It takes a profound understanding of leverage, as well as great courage, to be a successful LBO entrepreneur. Similarly, your experience and your character may cause you to reject certain GEOs, or to take them into very serious consideration.

# 6

# Predicting Entrepreneurial Success: The DEJ Factors

You undoubtedly have *insights* into entrepreneurial opportunities. You may also get an *inspiration* for a new business. How can you determine which insights you should pursue and which ones you should ignore? Are there any indicators that will help you decide which entrepreneurial opportunities to seize and which ones to pass over?

The answer is yes. As a potential entrepreneur, you can predict your eventual success or failure by counting the number of DEJ (Demonstrable Economic Justification) factors in your business idea. Here are the eight DEJ factors:

1. Existence of a large number of receivers
2. Homogeneity of receivers
3. Existence of qualified receivers
4. Existence of competent providers
5. Absence of institutional barriers to entry
6. "Hey, it really works!" factor
7. Invisibility
8. Optimum price–cost relationship

We will examine each of these eight factors shortly.

The beauty of the DEJ-factor system is its absolute infallibility: if you assess your entrepreneurial idea carefully and count the existing DEJ factors honestly, your prediction of future success will be surprisingly accurate. The more DEJ factors you can count, the more successful your company will be:

- A new company is super DEJ if it has all eight DEJ factors.
- A business is majority DEJ if it has all but one of the DEJ factors.
- A marginal DEJ company has only six of the eight DEJ factors.
- An enterprise is low DEJ if it possesses five or fewer DEJ factors.

### The Super DEJ Company

If your business idea possesses all eight DEJ factors, you should run, not walk, toward the launch, for yours is a super DEJ company and, as such, it is almost sure to solve a problem for a large number of people and make you very wealthy. Another virtue of the super DEJ company is that it does not require a great deal of venture capital. This sort of enterprise addresses a problem so large, and provides a solution—or a delivery system—so unique that it can be launched largely with customer financing. Because you will have to share the ownership and the profits with only a few venture capitalists, you will become wealthy in three to five years.

### The Majority DEJ Company

If your entrepreneurial idea has seven of the eight DEJ factors, you should vigorously pursue it. Because it is a majority DEJ idea, it has a very high probability of success. However, it will require a considerable amount of venture capital, perhaps ten times more than a super DEJ company would need. The rate of return on a majority DEJ company will be lower than that of a super DEJ business, and this applies not only to the return on capital but to the return on your time and labor as well.

### The Marginal DEJ Enterprise

An entrepreneurial opportunity that possesses six of the eight DEJ factors is likely to be only marginally successful. You should consider it very carefully before launching it, because it will require two to three times more venture capital than a majority DEJ company without offering the high probability of success.

## The Low DEJ Company

If you can count only five or fewer DEJ factors, you should forget that business idea. Such an enterprise would require an impossibly large amount of capital and would have little chance of success. By launching a low DEJ company you would be likely to waste your time and your investors' capital.

Let's examine each of the eight DEJ factors and see what it is about them that makes them so fundamental to a successful entrepreneurial company.

## EXISTENCE OF A LARGE NUMBER OF RECEIVERS

The problem you choose to solve must affect a large number of people. This means that there should be a large number of selling sites for your product or service and a relatively high price. Before launching or investing in a new company, I apply the big-$P$ test to find out if the business offers at least $1 billion in annual sales. To measure the size of the $P$, I multiply the number of selling sites by the price that people are likely to pay for the solution. Let's say, for example, that you have chosen to solve a problem that affects 500,000 Americans a year. You now determine that those who suffer from this problem would be willing to pay $3,000 for an effective, convenient, painless, nontoxic solution. A little calculating will tell you that $P$ equals $1.5 billion per annum—a very good-sized $P$.

You want to solve a problem that affects large numbers of people, because the payoff to society, to you, your entrepreneurial team, and your investors will be significantly greater than it would be for a smaller problem.

A company rarely achieves more than a ten percent share of any market, including those it creates, but ten percent of a very large market represents an attractive entrepreneurial opportunity. Let's look at the figures: ten percent of a $1 billion market means $100 million in annual revenues for a new company and roughly the same in market value—frequently more, if the profits are relatively high. Let's assume that you raise $1 million in venture capital for your new business and that the venture capitalist ends up with ten percent ownership: ten percent of $100 million is $10 million, or a tenfold return on capital in five to seven years, the normal length of time required to build $100 million in sales. Measuring this another way, let's assume that you persuade a corporate achiever to join your new company for ten percent ownership and that he or she attracts three or four key middle managers for an aggregate five percent ownership. After dilution, they might get ten percent ownership as well, or $10 million in value, a handsome payoff for managers who have left safe, stable corporate positions to take a chance on your entrepreneurial venture.

To place in proper perspective the word "large" as it applies to problems or markets, here is a list of ten U.S. and foreign markets with sales figures to indicate the size of each:

*Exhibit 6.1. Sizes of Ten Markets*

| Industry | 1985 Sales (Wholesale) ($000,000's) |
|---|---|
| 1. Automobiles | $ 99,873 |
| 2. Health and medical services | 466,000 |
| 3. Advertising (expenditures) | 104,000 |
| 4. Newspapers | 22,938 |
| 5. Movies (box office receipts) | 3,885 |
| 6. Computers | 65,800 |
| 7. Management consulting | 34,591 |
| 8. Athletic goods | 3,377 |
| 9. Trucks and bus bodies | 6,678 |
| 10. Life insurance (premium receipts) | 163,100 |

Source: U.S. Department of Commerce *Industrial Outlook*, 1986.

A ten percent market share of any of these ten markets represents a large company. Moreover, providing ancillary products and services to the members of these markets also represents a large entrepreneurial opportunity.

## HOMOGENEITY OF RECEIVERS

Entrepreneurial opportunities are greater if all of the receivers need the same solution. If the solution must be customized for each receiver, the problem probably does not represent an entrepreneurial opportunity. For example, cosmetic surgery is a solution that must be customized for each receiver. But repairing damaged vehicles is a fairly standard solution that has been provided entrepreneurially by Midas Muffler Shops; Meineke Mufflers, Inc.; Earl Scheib, Inc.; and other automobile repair chains.

Finding standardized solutions to human problems is somewhat more difficult than finding standardized solutions to industrial problems, because humans like to have choices. As an entrepreneur you can satisfy the need for choice in one of two ways: by offering various models of your product, or by changing your product as your market changes.

## Providing Various Models

To provide your receivers with a choice, while at the same time producing standardized products or services, you may decide to offer different varieties or models. Car manufacturers do this by producing sedans, convertibles, and station wagons. Some of them go even further by offering vehicles in different colors, with various available options, and at a wide range of prices. Other companies may offer just three models: small, medium, and large, for instance. Burger King successfully marketed hamburgers with the slogan "Have it your way," allowing consumers to select their own condiments. By stressing this freedom of choice, Burger King took a significant piece of the fast hamburger market away from McDonald's, the industry leader.

The need for choice can be a disadvantage, however. Computer software entrepreneurs have faced a sizable problem because of the absence of standardization among the various personal computers used in the home market. Because all software cannot be used on all computers, manufacturers typically customize their product to run on the three most popular PCs: IBM, Apple, and Commodore. The cost of doing this, however, is three times greater than it would be if the computer industry had a standard. As a result, entrepreneurial fortunes will probably not materialize in the home computer software market until a standard develops among PC manufacturers.

## Changing the Product to Suit a Changing Market

Standards can change, and do so rather abruptly. Apparel manufacturers must be alert to sudden swings in trends and tastes in order to produce garments that appeal to the greatest number of people. Standards last perhaps one or two seasons in the women's apparel market. As a result, a large number of company failures occur in that market. In the men's apparel market, standards last much longer. Therefore, entrepreneurs seeking to establish companies in the men's apparel field may attempt to introduce new standards. Ralph Lauren succeeded with his Polo line and then successfully diversified into women's apparel and home furnishings as well.

Radio stations, like apparel manufacturers, frequently change in order to keep up with the shifts in listeners' taste. A middle-of-the-road music station might change to a country-and-western format. A 1940s pop station might move forward in time to 1970s soft rock. An oldies-but-goodies broadcasting company might switch to talk radio, and so forth.

In studying a problem, you must be meticulous in your research and investigation to determine that the need for your solution is indeed fairly standard. If it is not, you could waste a great deal of capital.

## EXISTENCE OF QUALIFIED RECEIVERS

If people do not perceive that they have a problem, they are not likely to purchase a solution for it. It is the plight of many entrepreneurs to create solutions for problems which are not apparent to the intended recipients. In order to rescue their companies, entrepreneurs raise venture capital and spend it on creating "problem awareness." Some advertising people have become highly skilled at creating public awareness of problems, usually through a blitz of problem-awareness advertisements. Let's look at one of this century's most successful problem-awareness ad campaigns: Gene Lasker's ads for the Warner-Lambert mouthwash known as Listerine.

One of the greatest selling points of Listerine mouthwash is that it solves the problem of bad breath. Years ago, however, there was no widespread public awareness of the need for a product designed to solve that problem. To create the necessary awareness, Lasker built an advertising campaign around a scientific-sounding Latinate word meaning "bad breath." Within a short time, that word, halitosis, was in everyone's vocabulary and so was the brand name Listerine. The mouthwash was appropriately packaged in a no-nonsense corrugated cardboard tube covered with pharmaceutical information and made to look like an industrial-strength solution to the terrible, scientifically named problem of halitosis ("Even your best friend won't tell you"). Once they had been made aware of their problem, the horrified public sought the solution—Listerine—found that it worked, and continued to use it. Today the product, still packaged like a weapon, owns fifty percent of the mouthwash market.

The Quaker Oats Company had to address a similar problem when it introduced its now famous breakfast cereal. People needed oatmeal, but they didn't know they needed it, and they had a deep and long-standing prejudice against oats, which they regarded as a food suitable only for farm animals. (Samuel Johnson was probably the first writer to give oats a bad press. In his widely used dictionary, he defined oats as "a grain which in England is generally given to horses." As late as 1910, a cartoon in *Cosmopolitan* showed a Yankee farmer who would eat oatmeal and then prance around the barnyard and drink from the horses' trough.)

How did the manufacturer of an oat cereal overcome this public relations problem? It employed three marketing ploys to change the image of oats. One was the use of the Quaker Man, a symbol of honesty and strength of character, whose picture still appears on oatmeal boxes. Another was the package: a cardboard tube that could be used for storage or as a children's toy when the cereal was gone. The third marketing strategy was an advertising campaign that emphasized the health benefits of eating oatmeal. "Oats give you strength," the ads said. "They stick to your ribs. They give you 'sizzle.' "

The marketing campaign succeeded, and the public began to buy and eat Quaker's oatmeal, but the Society of Friends—known as the Quakers—sued the company in 1915 in an attempt to stop it from using the word "Quaker." The suit was unsuccessful in every state except Indiana.

If a new company has seven out of eight DEJ factors, but is missing this particular one—existence of qualified receivers—it will unquestionably have to raise venture capital in order to mount a problem-awareness advertising campaign. Even then, advertising is not the all-purpose palliative that its proponents claim. Where dozens of providers make similar claims for their solutions, the potential buyers doubt all of them. This situation occurred in the business software market in 1984–1985 in the area of networks and datalinks between disparate computers. Very few valid products were sold because the claims created a cacophony of confusing sounds.

If you attempt to provide a solution to receivers who do not know they have the problem, you may be faced with no sales or with a very long time interval between start-up and sales. Unless you can come up with a brilliant advertising campaign such as the one created for Listerine in the 1950s, you should step back from the starting line and reexamine the problem you want to solve.

Let's suppose, however, that you have identified a large group of qualified receivers—people who have a problem and who know they have it. You can create an entrepreneurial success by providing information about this problem in circumstances where there are many people who are concerned with the problem, who want to know how other people are affected by it, and who are curious about all possible solutions to it. In a big-*P* situation such as this, you might succeed as a publishing entrepreneur, providing information about the problem. You can do this by means of newsletters and seminars, or other publishing ventures. This has been done so successfully and so frequently that I have included it among the twelve solution-delivery methods, which I'll explain in the next chapter.

Patrick J. McGovern is an entrepreneur of this type; he is, in fact, one of the most successful marketers of information in this country's history. His company, International Data Group, Inc. (IDG), gathers data on the computer industry and sells it at $25,000 per annum to IDG's market research retainer clients and via sixty-two different publications, including *ComputerWorld* whose 120,000 subscribers make it the largest specialty publication in the country. Although privately held by McGovern and his employees, IDG is estimated to be worth $375 million. McGovern launched IDG in 1964 when IBM owned a seventy-three percent share of the computer market. The other computer vendors had so few customers that they had not been able to learn what kinds of computers, peripheral equipment, and software computer users wanted.

McGovern perceived a need for information here. He sent a letter to twenty-five vendors offering to gather market research for a $15,000 fee. Eighteen of the computer manufacturers responded positively with payment in advance. Within three years McGovern's market research business was grossing $600,000, and he was searching for new ideas to expand revenues. This time he perceived a need among computer users for information about products and services that could be of benefit to them. The decision to launch *ComputerWorld* came two weeks before a Boston trade show in 1967. McGovern and his staff produced a sixteen-page tabloid and subscription materials. At the trade show, so many people paid for subscriptions to the weekly tabloid that *ComputerWorld* had sufficient capital to fund the cost of publishing the journal.

Another entrepreneur who has gathered and marketed information about a problem to people with the problem is Gloria Steinem, the founding entrepreneur of *Ms.* magazine. The problem that Steinem identified is sexism. *Ms.* addresses that problem in articles and editorials, and consumer products manufacturers who address various aspects of the problem find the magazine an attractive medium through which to reach female consumers.

People read magazines to garner information about a problem. When they want to *share* information about the same problem or gain information from experts firsthand, they may attend a seminar. The conference, trade show, and seminar industry in the United States generated record revenues in 1984.

One of the most successful seminar entrepreneurs is Sheldon Adelson, who founded the Interface Group, Inc., in 1971 in order to promote COMDEX, the largest computer industry trade show in the world. Adelson charges vendors approximately $15,000 to display their wares in small booths on the exhibit floor. Customers are charged a $25 entrance fee. More than 150,000 people attended the 1984 COMDEX trade show. In addition, COMDEX offers one hundred seminars with some of the industry's leading managers and consultants as speakers. The Interface Group's revenues are estimated at approximately $175 million per annum. Providers of information, as we shall see, generally create multiple channels through which to sell their information as well as multiple ancillary services that bring in considerable additional revenue. The Interface Group, for example, is also in the travel agency business, a spin-off of its years of booking hotels for its trade shows.

People who have a problem and know they have it, then, are eager to buy information about it, and their curiosity will demand that this information be made available in various formats. Numerous multimillionaire publishing entrepreneurs serve as proof that information provided to needy receivers is extremely valuable.

## EXISTENCE OF COMPETENT PROVIDERS

*Competence* is the ability to perform a task satisfactorily. It means being able to get the job done. It does *not* mean getting it done better or faster than anyone else, and that point is worth remembering.

This fourth DEJ factor requires that competent sales people be hired or commissioned to deliver satisfaction to the customers. As an entrepreneur, you don't need to hire Nobel laureates to sell your high-technology products, nor do you need to hire David Ogilvy to develop an eye patch campaign like the one he devised for Hathaway shirts. You need a sales force that is competent, not perfect. In fact, if your product is so complicated that it takes a mechanical genius to demonstrate it, your customers will probably be afraid to buy it. A good rule of thumb is this: the higher the technology, the less sophisticated the sales method should be. Federal Express Corporation provides an example of unsophisticated sales techniques. The company was founded in 1973 to provide overnight delivery of small packages throughout the United States and Canada. It has an elegantly integrated air-ground transportation system. However, the company was unable to get its revenues up high enough to cover its constantly increasing expenses until it developed a very basic sales slogan: "Absolutely positively overnight," stressing its competence in order to attract customers.

Competent sellers enjoy talking with their customers. They listen to them and learn what their needs are. Then they respond to those needs by providing the kind of solution each customer requires. This applies not only to the installation of the product but to after-sale service and support as well. When a transaction is performed competently, both the giver and the receiver are satisfied.

## ABSENCE OF INSTITUTIONAL BARRIERS TO ENTRY

The federal government acts as a tollgate operator, charging entry fees of one sort or another to those who want to gain entry into various enterprises. State and city governments have picked up the habit, and they, too, charge tolls and levy taxes on "everything that moves, breathes, or grows." In the name of protecting us from ourselves the federal government has created agencies to protect us from unfair labor practices, dirty air, unclean water, cars that pollute the air, airplane crashes, and harmful pharmaceutical products and medical equipment. These safeguards may be worth the price, you say? Try raising $54 million and spending eight years of your life developing a product. That is the average cost and length of time required to launch a new pharmaceutical product and obtain approval to market it from the U.S. Food & Drug Administration.

In order to carry freight in Boeing 727s, Fredrick W. Smith had to seek approval of the Federal Aviation Administration, a process that required eighteen months during which time his company, Federal Express, accumulated over $5 million in losses.

Why do governments erect barriers in front of those who want to provide product A and service B, while letting the providers of product Y and service Z regulate themselves? Why is a venture capitalist free of regulation while a commercial banker is required to maintain a sixteen percent reserve for every dollar he has on deposit? Why can that banker sell stocks or IRAs to individuals while a venture capitalist can solicit capital only from the very wealthy? Are venture capital investments riskier than commercial loans? Strange are the mysteries that prompt the government to place a tollgate here and allow free passage there.

Institutional barriers can cost the entrepreneur a substantial amount of capital. Genentech, Inc., was founded in 1976 by Robert A. Swanson and Herbert W. Boyer for the purpose of developing, producing, and marketing pharmaceuticals produced by recombinant DNA technology in order to attempt to effectively treat dwarfism, diabetes, and cancer. In 1985, nearly ten years after its launch, Genentech received approval from the FDA to market its first product, one that treats dwarfism effectively. To get this far, Genentech had to raise $125 million in venture capital.

Real estate developers, whose new commercial and residential projects are given the most perfunctory review by city zoning boards, face no serious institutional barriers to entrepreneuring. The result is more expensive rather than less expensive housing, and urban sprawl. Meanwhile, health-sciences entrepreneurs who could be helping millions of people, line up behind tollgates. People die and suffer while the necessary dollars are raised to pay the high tolls. Real estate developers and their investors have been receiving a ten percent credit against taxable income for their investments, but health-sciences entrepreneurs and their investors must bear the full risk. Real estate developers and their investors are able to depreciate the cost of their investments over a fairly short period of time, thus receiving back the full amount of their investment, plus the amount they borrow, in the form of tax savings. Health-sciences entrepreneurs and their investors are not able to depreciate the cost of their investment. Thus health-sciences entrepreneurs must contend with a very expensive toll in the middle of their highway and fewer breaks for their investors relative to certain other investment alternatives such as real estate. To the millions of victims of heart disease, cancer, and diabetes for whom treatment is thereby delayed, the government's choice of highways on which to erect tollgates must seem diabolical.

If you are intent on solving problems in areas where there are institutional barriers to entry, you should know going in that the venture will require extra time and capital. This means that your ownership and eventual wealth are likely to be significantly less than they would be if there were no tollgates blocking your entry.

## *"HEY, IT REALLY WORKS" FACTOR*

This DEJ factor can exist only if your product or service is so excellent that the receivers become excited enough to tell others about it. When that happens ("Hey, it really works!"), you will benefit from word-of-mouth advertising that is very effective and will not cost you a cent. One customer uses your product and finds it a perfect solution to his particular problem. He tells three friends, each of whom tells two friends, and so on. As the word spreads, the testimonials from satisfied users will most often include an explanation of how your product works and directions to the nearest outlet where it can be purchased.

It is my feeling that if a new venture requires significant advertising dollars in order to generate sales, it is not likely to be successful. If the intended receivers are aware that they have a specific need, and if the need is homogeneous and felt by a large number of people, then they will pay for the solution in advance. If the receivers doubt the solution will be effective, doubt the entrepreneur's ability to deliver it, or are skeptical in other ways, they are likely to pay only after they have received the product and used it for a short time. If advertising is required in your new venture, you will have to raise a substantial amount of venture capital, thus lowering your own rate of return and casting doubt on your investors' return.

There are exceptions, of course. When two or more entrepreneurs create a similar solution at the same time, for example, advertising will be required to differentiate the solutions. This situation occurred in the personal computer industry in the early 1980s when hundreds of new companies were formed and abundantly funded to offer virtually identical software to the owners of personal computers. Some entrepreneurs spent millions of dollars of venture capital to advertise new software products *that did not yet exist.* Some of these entrepreneurs ran out of capital before bringing a product to market. These software companies became known as producers of "vaporware," because their products vaporized before they were produced. The best known vaporware company, Knoware, Inc., received more than $5 million from some of the most respected venture capitalists in the country.

The computer magazines swelled in size with the software entrepreneurs' advertisements. One month *Byte* magazine reached 640 pages, a thickness previously achieved only by *Vogue.*

You can avoid this kind of problem by getting a word-of-mouth campaign started. How should you go about this project? One way is to get your product reviewed in a trade journal. Nowadays, there seems to be a clutch of critics for just about everything on the market: movies, television shows, computer software, automobiles, pharmaceutical products, and the list goes on. It is the job of these critics to judge the products of entrepreneurs, and their published or broadcast reviews constitute a noninstitutional barrier of sorts to entry. The reviewers do not collect a monetary toll; rather, their impartiality and judgment are the barriers. A favorable review from one of these critics can be of inestimable value to an entrepreneurial company. Many successful entrepreneurs "play to the press" in order to generate a plethora of favorable reviews during the launching of a new product, and favorable word-of-mouth advertising to coincide with a marketing campaign. The sales staff can cite the favorable reviews and tell the receivers that "Hey, it really works!"

## INVISIBILITY

Anything worth doing is also worth duplicating. A successful entrepreneurial innovation will be copied, because it is the nature of people to avoid risk by doing something that someone else has already done successfully. What better way to minimize risk than to copy an effective solution, change it slightly, then offer it to the same receivers who bought the original? Large companies have more capital to sustain a competitive battle with entrepreneurial companies; therefore, large companies are usually the predators and entrepreneurial companies are the prey in the competitive jungle.

If you want to prevent others from duplicating your product or service, you will have to find ways to remain invisible to the predators. How can you make your entrepreneurial company invisible to potential copycats? There are several steps you can take:

1. Don't advertise your product or service. Rely instead on a positive word-of-mouth campaign.

2. Don't raise capital by means of a public offering until you are in the growth stage, with all of your key functions covered by experienced managers and with enough capital on hand to defend your market position. An early initial public offering gives potential predators much information that should remain invisible—financial details and names of key customers and important suppliers, for example.

3. If you have applied for a patent, add components to the patent application which will make it difficult to copy.

4. Impress on your employees the importance of loyalty and secrecy. Ask them not to describe the company or their work to anyone except potential receivers and even then only on a need-to-know basis.

Many successful entrepreneurs are intensely private and do not permit members of their staff to grant interviews. IBM Corporation, the longest-running entrepreneurial show in the American economy, maintains such high standards of privacy that when you call an IBM manager to check the references of a former employee, the only information you will normally receive is "Yes, that person was employed at IBM." Henry E. Singleton, the founding entrepreneur of Teledyne, Inc., is nicknamed "the Sphinx" by Wall Street securities analysts, because of his near legendary unwillingness to give interviews to the press. In fact it is difficult to find a successful entrepreneurial company that has made itself highly visible or that had an initial public offering as a raw start-up and set forth its business plan in glowing detail for all to see. Invisibility, in other words, is highly valued by those entrepreneurs who wish to avoid having their products duplicated. These people understand that the only thing that should be made visible is the solution.

## OPTIMUM PRICE-COST RELATIONSHIP

In simple terms, this DEJ factor means that the gift should bear a high gross profit margin. However, many products and services are leased or made available to customers on terms and conditions other than straight sale; thus, the operating statement line item "gross profit margin" is inappropriate. "Optimum price–cost relationship" conveys the thought more accurately.

Many entrepreneurs give little thought to the method of conveying their product or service to their receivers. Selling a product for a negotiated price is but one method of receiving payment. There are many others, including the following:

- Monthly rental
- Lease with purchase option
- Sale with service contract
- Sale with disposable trail
- Subscription
- Meter or toll (per-use charge)
- Facilities management contract
- License
- OEM agreement
- Refundable deposit
- Refundable bond with accumulating interest
- Franchise arrangement: payment for geographical exclusivity and rights to the trademark plus royalty tied to sales
- Dealership arrangement

The methods of receiving consideration for providing a solution to a problem are increasing year by year as entrepreneurs devote more thought to the subject. Some of the more interesting pricing methods are discussed in Chapter 7. It is sufficient to point out here that the price of the solution should be substantially greater—certainly more than 500 percent—than the cost of producing it. The reasons for a large markup over cost are several. The most important are:

- You can always come down in price but never go up.
- When competition enters the marketplace that you have created, it will certainly do so at a price lower than yours, or at the same price, but with more features.
- Most products and services have a relatively short life, after which time they are replaced with a "new, improved model." The original product is then sold at a reduced price in order to dispose of

accumulated inventory. The higher your initial price the greater your profit when you discount the initial model.

- Price is a means of presenting an image of value. The higher the price, the greater the perception of value.

## A MODEL SUPER DEJ COMPANY

The eight DEJ factors are the fundamental requirements of successful entrepreneurship. You cannot play the entrepreneurial game successfully unless you thoroughly understand them. If you leap into an entrepreneurial company with fewer than six of the eight DEJ factors, your company will almost certainly fail. If your venture has only six of the eight factors, you will require several million dollars of venture capital, and you will have a low probability of success. With seven DEJ factors, your chance of success increases and the venture capital requirement decreases. With all eight DEJ factors, however, your probability of success is extremely high and your need for venture capital relatively small.

If you have all eight DEJ factors, you might be able to turn a relatively small investment into a very large fortune. H. Ross Perot was able to do just that with his eight-DEJ company, creating the largest amount of wealth in the shortest period of time with the smallest initial capital investment of any entrepreneur on record. Perot formed Electronic Data Systems Corporation (EDS) in 1964 with $24,000 and built it up to a valuation of $1.5 billion in five years, using customer financing as his principal revenue source.

Because no outside equity capital was required, Perot owned most of EDS's common stock and became a billionaire within five years after start-up. The problem that EDS addressed was very large. Although this partially explains the enormous wealth created by EDS, another factor of equal importance is that EDS possessed all eight DEJ factors. It is possible for entrepreneurs to replicate EDS, but EDS should be regarded as the perfect facilities-management company, and we can learn from studying it as a model of perfection. Before we examine EDS's DEJ factors, however, let's take a moment to study the way Perot went about establishing his entrepreneurial company.

An exceptionally good IBM mainframe computer salesman, Perot had sold his full year's quota by February 1964 and couldn't earn any additional money no matter how many more computers he sold, so he left IBM. Then he called on his large customers—including Blue Cross/Blue Shield and Pepsi Cola Bottlers of Texas—and asked them if they were getting their data processing needs satisfied. They said no. (At that time data processing meant accounts receivable, inventory, accounts payable, payroll, and general ledger.) Perot learned that his first client's annual data processing budget was $1 million.

"And you cannot generate receivables, payables, inventory, payroll, or general ledger reports?" asked Perot, bemused.

"No, we cannot."

Perot said, "Why don't you put the data processing personnel on my payroll and sell or lease me the computers and peripheral equipment? Pay me the $1 million you are now spending for data processing, and I will deliver the reports you need when you need them. If I can do the job for less than $1 million, I'll make money. If it costs me more than $1 million, I'll lose money."

The client, eager to justify his new data processing division and responsibility, said yes.

Thus was born a new business form, or solution delivery method: the facilities-management company. (This method of delivery is discussed in detail in Chapter 7.)

Perot then approached client two and made the same offer: to provide a data processing solution for the price of the data processing problem. The client agreed to have EDS manage its data processing facility, and it paid EDS $1 million and transferred to EDS its personnel and equipment.

EDS's second client needed the same kind of reports that the company was generating for its first client (*homogeneous receivers*), so EDS sold the computers and peripheral equipment received from the second client and terminated some of the personnel. Its revenues were thus $2 million per annum, while its profits approached $1 million.

Perot then approached his third and fourth clients and made them the same offer. EDS's revenues grew, and its profits grew even faster. Perot merged EDS into General Motors in 1985 for $2.5 billion in General Motors common stock. Some analysts predict that he will end up running the automaker.

Let's take a look at the eight DEJ factors of Perot's company at start-up.

## DEJ 1: Large Number of Receivers

Perot set out to solve a problem: satisfying his clients' data processing needs. The number of potential buyers—corporations and institutions—who shared that problem was in excess of 3,000. Assuming that each one had a data processing budget of $1 million per annum, the market size for EDS's solution was $3 billion per annum, and no competitor was within two years of sharing a piece of the pie. (More than any other single circumstance, this explains why EDS's initial public offering was at a common stock price in excess of 115 times earnings, a then unheard of figure.) DEJ factor 1, then, was firmly in place.

## DEJ 2: Homogeneity of Receivers

The problem that EDS solved was essentially the same for all buyers, with minor differences in degree or severity. The solution did not have to be tailor-made or customized for each buyer. Selling "off the racks" is cheaper and provides more rapid cash flow than selling custom-made services or products.

## DEJ 3: Existence of Qualified Receivers

Corporate data processing inefficiency was a very real problem. Buyers did not have to be told they had a problem; they knew they had a problem, knew they had to pay for a solution, and were able to pay for a solution. A minimum amount of buyer education was required.

## DEJ 4: Existence of Competent Providers

Perot hired managers who were skilled in providing solutions to the problems of EDS's customers. Perot himself was a skilled salesman, and he hired personnel in his image. He was competitive, and so were his employees.

## DEJ 5: Absence of Institutional Barriers to Entry

EDS's receivers were not organized. They belonged to no association. No regulatory body such as the American Medical Association or the Civil Aeronautics Board held authority over their activities. The receivers would not have to seek permission or clarification from any outside institution. In short, there were no barriers to EDS's entry into business.

## DEJ 6: "Hey, It Really Works!" Factor

News of EDS's success in solving the electronic data processing problem was passed along from one receiver to another by word of mouth, the least expensive and most effective means of advertising.

## DEJ 7: Invisibility

EDS operated quietly, without fanfare or publicity. It did not advertise or promote itself heavily. Because it did not gain attention, competitors could not copy it. As a result, EDS remained the only important facilities-management company for nearly ten years. By the time other companies began to enter the field in the 1970s, Perot had achieved his entrepreneurial fortune.

## DEJ 8: Optimum Price–Cost Relationship

The price of EDS's solution was equal to the cost of the problem—that is, the buyer's data processing budget. EDS could not be accused of charging an excessively high price because the buyer had been paying the same price for his problem that EDS was asking him to pay for the solution. If the same $1 million that had caused problems could now result in a solution, the buyer was $1 million ahead.

In Chapter 7 we will discuss the various ways in which entrepreneurs can deliver their solutions to receivers. Among these solution delivery methods is the one that Perot pioneered: facilities management.

# 7

## Solution Delivery Methods

Now that you have examined your entrepreneurial opportunity to make sure it has enough DEJ factors to succeed, your next step in the entrepreneurial game is to select the solution delivery method (SDM) that you will use to convey your solution to the problem. To make the solution available to the greatest possible number of people, you may prefer to select one primary SDM and several ancillary SDMs.

Here are the twelve solution delivery methods:

1. Facilities management
2. Prepaid subscription
3. Franchising
4. Party plan
5. Celebrity-endorsed consumer product
6. Consumer product
7. High-technology
8. Cookie cutter
9. Capital equipment
10. Tollgate

11. Newsletter-seminar
12. Franchise on OPA (other people's assets)

Let's review each of these delivery methods in detail. Later in this chapter we'll talk about using more than one SDM at a time.

## FACILITIES MANAGEMENT

The facilities-management entrepreneur agrees to manage a certain facility for a corporation, institution, or government agency at a price equal to what the client is currently paying for that service. The entrepreneur assumes full responsibility for the direct expenses and overhead of the facility. If he is able to deliver the solution for less than it cost the corporation, the resulting profit is his reward. If, on the other hand, he spends more than the allotted amount to get the job done, he must sustain the loss himself.

Jack Massey, an entrepreneur with long experience and a record of great success, launched a facilities-management business in 1983. Known as Corrections Corporation of America, it has as its purpose the management of prisons under contract. For starters, Massey offered to run the prison system of the state of Tennessee for the current budget of $150 million per annum, with the understanding that if he could manage it for less than that amount, the money saved would be CCA's profit. The beauty of this SDM, of course, is that the taxpayers of the state of Tennessee couldn't lose. Their prison system, no matter what it cost CCA, could not possibly cost them more than the $150 million agreed on. Furthermore, they could rest in the knowledge that they had put their prisons in the hands of a businessman with a track record of success: Massey is the only entrepreneur ever to take three companies to the New York Stock Exchange; furthermore, he co-founded Kentucky Fried Chicken with an investment of $500,000 and later sold it for $250 million.

The founder of the facilities-management SDM—who may not have realized he was a pioneer—was H. Ross Perot, whom we discussed in Chapter 6. A close study of Perot's operation will help you gain a clear understanding of the way the facilities-management SDM works.

This SDM has been used in markets other than data processing and prison management. Money management companies, for example, have used it frequently and with considerable success. One example is the investment department of Chemical Bank, New York, which is responsible for $9.5 billion in assets under management for trust customers. This department is managed by a team that is employed by and has an equity interest in Favia, Hill, Inc., a management company. James A. Favia and his partner, John Hill, once headed Chemical Bank's investment department. They negotiated with the top brass at the bank, and agreed to run the $9.5 billion investments department as proper fiduciaries. They would do so for the bank's budget, but in a different entity—not as employees of the bank but as stockholders of a new money management company, Favia, Hill, Inc. Now Favia and Hill can sell their stock-picking skills to new clients, grow their company to any size they like, and take it public or sell it back to Chemical Bank or the highest bidder.

How might this work out? Assume that a money management firm charges its customers one half of one percent of total assets under management. Then a company with $3 billion under management has gross income of $15 million. If 100 people are employed to manage $3 billion, at an average salary of $75,000 per annum, and if another $500,000 per annum is spent on investigation costs, then the net profit to the owners of the company is $7 million. If the assets under management double to $6 billion and if only twenty-five employees are added to the payroll, net profits to the owners will grow to $20 million. An owner of ten percent of the stock of the money management company would receive a dividend of $2 million for doing the same job he or she once earned bank wages for doing.

Favia, Hill is one of many money management departments of commercial banks that have used the facilities-management SDM to establish themselves as separate companies. The venture capital industry is composed of some 625 firms, about five percent of which were launched using the facilities-management SDM. The venture capital arm of Bank of America, for example, became Merrill Pickard Anderson & Eyres. The fashion industry is dotted with designers who design apparel lines under contract to manufacturers as well as for their own label.

Federal and state governments are beginning to express interest in facilities management. The agencies that they seem most willing to spin off to entrepreneurs are the less attractive ones such as waste removal and prison management. But as the entrepreneurial revolution builds up a head of steam, and as more and more people select entrepreneurship as a career, governments will sell off many more agencies to entrepreneurs. Even the pork barrel agencies—the ones where cousins of campaign workers are given jobs—will someday be spun off to entrepreneurs. These include highway construction and the management of schools, bridges, libraries, and hospitals.

In the private sector, the possibilities of establishing a facilities management entrepreneurial company are myriad. Regardless of what field you now work in, you would do well to take a look at the various ways in which you could put this SDM to work for you.

### Putting Facilities Management to Work

So far we have talked about facilities management in detail only in connection with data processing, money management, and fashion. Let's take a moment to see how you could make use of this SDM in your own area of expertise. Here are some possibilities in three widely divergent fields.

**Journalism.** Could you transform yourself from a journalist into a facilities-management entrepreneur? Yes. Here's a step-by-step guide to doing just that:

1. Get together with the other members of your department—let's say you work for the sports section—and calculate your departmental budget.
2. Decide whether you could produce the sports section for less than the amount the company is now spending.
3. Discuss the possibility of launching new sports publications or managing the sports sections of other newspapers. Calculate what this would cost and what your revenues would be.
4. Negotiate a facilities management contract with your employer.
5. Raise $100,000 in backup venture capital to demonstrate that your new company has adequate net worth and is acting responsibly.

**Corporate Planning.** If you are a corporate planner, you might proceed this way:

1. Meet with the other members of your department and calculate the departmental budget.
2. Estimate additional revenues you might bring in by attracting corporations as clients. (Remember all those job offers you and your fellow team members have turned down over the years.)
3. Negotiate a facilities management contract with your employer.
4. Raise $100,000 in venture capital to serve as a safety net.
5. Line up additional revenue-generating clients.

**Human Resources.** You work in the human resources department at a large corporation. Part of your job is to manage the health and life insurance of thousands of people. You could use the facilities-management SDM to break away from the corporation and become an entrepreneur:

1. Carefully study the possibility of forming a separate company to provide health insurance to your employer and to other corporations.
2. Raise enough venture capital to serve as a cushion.
3. Negotiate a facilities management contract with the corporation for which you now work.
4. Sell your health maintenance organization plan to several other corporations to provide an initial cash flow base.

This SDM is likely to succeed for a team of people who have worked well together in a large corporation. By becoming facilities management entrepreneurs, these people can continue to serve that corporation as well as many others, with the resulting profits falling into their own cash register instead of someone else's.

Opportunities for facilities management entrepreneurs exist in many "smart money" fields. Here are just a few of them:

- Publishing
- Broadcasting
- Entertainment
- Consumer nondurables
- Health sciences
- Insurance

You should regard facilities management as the primary SDM and as a financing technique as well. Keep in mind, however, that if you wish to succeed with this method, you should launch swiftly into other revenue-generating channels and ancillary SDMs to create additional cash flow streams.

## PREPAID SUBSCRIPTION

The prepaid subscription SDM requires very little start-up capital and has one of the highest probabilities of success. The newest group of entrepreneurs to use this extraordinary SDM are in the health insurance field. Their companies are called health maintenance organizations (HMOs). Clients pay about $60 a month to belong to an HMO, and in return the HMO provides all of the health-care services the subscribers need, including physicians, medication, and hospital care as long as they are HMO members. The HMOs contract for the services of doctors, hospitals, and other health-care providers by payment in advance. The contracts are based on a per capita fee rather than fee for service.

Knowing its costs (having prepaid the providers), the HMOs then try to maintain a high level of wellness among their subscribers so that they can avoid using the health-care providers. They do this by scheduling frequent checkups, encouraging aerobic exercise and good nutrition, discouraging smoking, and providing stress management.

The HMOs use the subscribers' prepayments as operating capital, thus reducing their need to raise venture capital.

Alas the HMOs lack one DEJ factor: they do face institutional barriers to entry. These companies are regulated by federal and state governmental agencies, and obtaining a license is a time-consuming and expensive process. Should you wish to become an HMO entrepreneur, you might choose not to form a new one. Instead, you could acquire an existing not-for-profit HMO, convert it to a for-profit HMO, post the license with the state, and operate it with its existing, experienced management team. The acquisition cost would be *zero* because nobody owns an HMO. The license is actually money—approximately $1 million—placed in a savings instrument as a reserve to protect the subscribers in the event the HMO should fail. Thus because they're missing one critical DEJ factor, HMOs need about $1 million or more to begin operating on a for-profit basis. Because the upside is very high, however, many investors are eager to ante up venture capital to HMOs.

The prepaid subscription SDM has been used in industries other than health care. The father of membership merchandising is Sol Price who in 1975 formed the Price Company, which sells consumer nondurable merchandise in large warehouses to members of the Price Club. Individuals and businesses become members of the Price Club by paying an annual membership fee of $25 per person. For an additional $10, a member may designate two additional buyers. Price Club members are offered goods at substantial discounts. Price has 170,000 wholesale members and 800,000 group members shopping at his twenty stores. That represents $13.5 million in annual prepaid membership fees, or $600,000 per store. A successful entrepreneur can leverage $13.5 million into a fair amount of debt financing to grow his business, and Price has done just that.

Other companies that have used prepaid subscriptions as a solution delivery modality include the following:

1. Franklin Mint, which markets collectibles via direct mail
2. Book-of-the-Month Club, Inc.
3. Commerce Clearing House Corporation, a daily compilation of court decisions sold to lawyers
4. Harry & David, a fruit-of-the-month business
5. Columbia Record Club, Inc., a tape-of-the-month business

Can you think of some information that would be salable to a large, homogeneous, qualified group of people? The information should solve a specific problem that is sufficiently serious to make people willing to pay for it in advance. There are numerous means of strategically selling information where the customer will pay in advance. One may be appropriate for you.

## FRANCHISING

According to the Department of Commerce, total retail sales of franchised companies were approximately $530 billion in 1985, or roughly one third of all retail sales. Franchisees contributed 15 percent of the nation's GNP in 1985, and over 5.9 million people were employed by 454,000 retail establishments. The growth of franchising has been remarkable. Total retail sales of franchised companies were $321 billion in 1982, and $168 million in 1973.

Retail franchising works because it is based on the first law of entrepreneurship ($V = P \times S \times E$):

- The franchisor identifies a problem ($P$), creates an elegant solution ($S$), and provides training for the franchisee's managers ($E$).
- Franchisors prepare instructional material for franchisees with great attention to detail. Murphy's Law—everything that can go wrong will go wrong—applies among franchisees, and providing answers to franchisees' questions, no matter how minute, is of vital importance.
- Franchising is first and foremost a means of generating wealth ($V$) for the franchisor. Two to three years after launch, well-managed

franchisors normally go public and use part of the proceeds to acquire the most profitable franchisees. This provides an incentive to all franchisees that there is a capital gain opportunity available to them as well, via acquisition by the franchisor.

Franchising succeeds when the franchisor (1) optimizes *P, S,* and *E,* (2) pays very close attention to detail, and (3) recognizes that he or she must purchase the most profitable franchisees to demonstrate to all of them the wealth (as opposed to income) possibilities of their businesses. Franchisors fail for the same reasons that users of other SDMs fail: a zero value for *P, S,* or *E.*

Before launching a new company using the franchising SDM, you should examine in close detail the eight DEJ factors that relate to the *P* you have selected. That way you can avoid the sort of franchise that seems to stir the adrenalin of numerous entrepreneurs about once every ten years: the idea of establishing a new football league. Some years ago the World Football League was founded; more recently we saw the birth and death of the U.S. Football League. Exercise your entrepreneurial skills by examining these two leagues in terms of the DEJ factors they possessed. As you go through the list below, check off the DEJ factors for each of the two leagues:

| WFL | USFL | |
| --- | --- | --- |
| ___ | ___ | Large number of receivers |
| ___ | ___ | Homogeneity of receivers |
| ___ | ___ | Qualified receivers |
| ___ | ___ | Competent providers |
| ___ | ___ | Absence of institutional barriers to entry |
| ___ | ___ | "Hey, it really works!" factor |
| ___ | ___ | Invisibility |
| ___ | ___ | Optimum price–cost relationship |

How many DEJ factors did you check? If your answer is none, you are 100 percent correct. These two franchises had *no* demonstrable economic justification factors.

You might ask, why were they established? The answer: They were founded for three reasons, not a single one of which was a DEJ factor. Here are those reasons:

1. Mayors and councilmen in smaller cities wanted stadium rental fees and didn't care who filled the seats.

2. Wealthy real estate developers and others wanted the excitement of being in the benevolent order of rugged athletes, and liked the rapid depreciation characteristics of athletes as a form of tax shelter. (A football player depreciates in five years. Thus a five-year $5 million contract provides $2 million of depreciation in the first year, using the accelerated basis.)

3. Non-network television stations were willing to pay for the rights to broadcast the alternative league games.

Unused stadium capacity, love of sports, and tax shelter are not DEJ factors, however, and the alternative football leagues were doomed to failure from the beginning.

But all of this brings up another thought: athletes are not unlike members of an important revenue department of a large corporation—say, the investment department of a major money market bank. If the investment managers can negotiate a facilities management contract for themselves, why can't the players on a national football league team do the same thing? Instead of working for salaries, professional athletes will someday own themselves via facilities management contracts. It is inevitable.

Franchising began in 1851 when the I. W. Singer Company, manufacturer of the first sewing machine, was financially strapped. A hotshot salesman in Ohio was taking orders for sewing machines faster than Singer could supply them. He was earning $8,000 per annum, a princely sum in those days. Salesmen in Illinois and Michigan were doing almost as well. Out of desperation, I. W. Singer Company charged its salesmen a fee for the right to sell its sewing machines in designated territories, and the fees became Singer's capital. The salesmen were converted to dealers.

General Motors Corporation copied the Singer format in 1898, once again as a means to raise up-front financing. General Motors sold dealerships to bicycle shops and hardware stores, which sold cars as a sideline.

Thirty years later, Standard Oil converted its company-owned service stations to dealerships by leasing them to their operators. Intense price wars at the retail level had caused much revenue uncertainty for Standard Oil. If the service stations became dealers, Standard Oil could sell its oil at a fixed price.

In consumer nondurable products, the first dealerships were Coca Cola bottlers. The founders of Coca Cola in 1886 narrow-mindedly saw their product as a soda fountain–only idea. Two Chattanooga entrepreneurs, Benjamin Thomas and Joseph Whitehead, persuaded the president of Coca Cola to grant them a license to sell the product in bottles. Thomas and Whitehead were granted the bottling rights for most of the country.

When demand for Coca Cola grew, Thomas and Whitehead needed capital to respond effectively. They created franchises. In 1903, they sold thirty-two franchises; the next year forty-seven. By 1909, the number was approaching 400; and by 1919, there were 1,000 Coca Cola bottlers.

Franchising requires a modest amount of start-up capital. As little as $25,000 to $50,000 need be raised, for the purpose of vendor financing, to open a prototype store to test the concept, and to see what features the customers like best and least. The franchisor then sells the rights to open and operate identical stores in different regions. The franchisees pay for their franchises in advance and also pay a monthly royalty based on sales. In return, the franchisor agrees to provide management advice, national advertising, and other services. Frequently the franchisor, sitting on piles of cash, reacquires the successful franchisees because their profits are larger than their monthly royalties. In fact, many franchising companies have fallen apart when the franchisor went public and its founders became visibly wealthy while not sharing the wealth with the most profitable franchisees. Although an excellent SDM, franchising is first and foremost a financing strategy.

Can you name the franchises in your city? You probably have at least one of the following:

- Arthur Murray Dance Studio
- Century 21
- Computerland
- Culligan
- H&R Block
- Holiday Inns of America
- Kelly Girl
- Kentucky Fried Chicken
- Orkin Exterminating Company
- Pizza Hut

There are several variations on the franchising theme. Automobile and tire dealerships are a form of franchising. Several new religions and self-actualization groups, such as EST, have used the franchising solution method, as have diet and bingo centers. In computer retailing, the largest chains are Computerland Corporation and Entre Computer Corporation, where the franchisor and franchisees have been frequently in conflict over a failure to share the wealth.

## PARTY PLAN

This SDM has been underutilized, but for those who have adopted it—Tupperware Division of Dart-Kraft, Inc.; Mary Kay Cosmetics, Inc.; Discovery Toys, Inc.; Shaklee Corp.; Amway Corp.; Transart Industries, Inc.; and others—it has acted as a cash cow. In the party plan SDM, sometimes called in-home marketing, salespeople call on homemakers who then invite their friends to a party at their homes—a Tupperware party, for instance. The salesperson sets the products out and demonstrates them for the host and his or her friends. These products are not available in stores and are generally the kind of items that sell quickly once the customers have had a chance to see, touch, and smell them. Thus there is quite a bit of demonstrating, chatting, and experimenting at these product parties.

The salesperson writes invoices for each customer sale and promises shipment within three weeks or so. He or she accepts cash, checks, and credit cards. After the party, she phones the orders in to the company's warehouse. Checks are deposited the next day. Thus the party plan company has the use of the customers' cash for about three weeks.

The host and the salesperson both receive a commission of ten to fifteen percent; the district manager and the trainer-supervisor receive a smaller commission; and the regional manager receives an override on the sale as well. Very little product advertising is necessary in the party plan SDM, thus permitting these hefty commission structures.

Nevertheless, for the party plan SDM to succeed, the entrepreneurial company's product should be marked up in price at least tenfold over cost of goods sold. For example, a Transart framed print that sells in the home for $60 should cost Transart Industries, Inc., no more than $6 to produce. Naturally, this forces Transart to buy prints, mats, glass, and frames in large quantities in order to get its costs down to $6 per product. The commissions add up to approximately forty percent, and assuming a $2 freight or postage charge (borne by the customer), a transaction on one item might break down as follows:

| Retail price | | $62.00 |
|---|---|---|
| Commissions: | | |
| Hostess | $9.00 | |
| Salesperson | 9.00 | |
| District manager | 6.00 | |
| Regional manager | 3.00 | |
| Total commissions | | 27.00 |
| Cost of goods sold | | 6.00 |
| Freight | | 2.00 |
| Total expense | | $35.00 |
| Net income before company overhead | | $27.00 |

Mary Kay Ash is probably the best-known—and certainly the most written about—party plan entrepreneur in the United States today. The story of how she built a $5,000 personal-savings investment into the $300 million company known as Mary Kay Cosmetics, Inc., has been told too often to bear repeating here. Keep in mind, however, that part of Ash's success is attributable to her willingness to give to others. She starts by giving her salespeople the courage to leave their kitchens and the confidence to put the party plan SDM to work for them and for her. And she continues to give the kind of rewards that mean something to her people—including lavish financial rewards, glowing praise, and the famous pink Cadillacs that have become a Mary Kay trademark. This giving, as I've said before, is what entrepreneurship is all about.

Another party plan entrepreneur is Mary Carson, a Modesto, California, office worker who faced a problem because of the current passion for very long, well-manicured fingernails. Since she spent her workdays typing and using business machines, Carson was unable to cultivate fashionably long nails. She could have had artificial nails applied in a manicure salon, of course, but that was time-consuming and would have cost more than $300 a year. The only way to solve this problem, she decided, was to purchase inexpensive plastic nails and learn to lacquer and apply them herself.

It was at this point that Carson began to think like an entrepreneur. Instead of seeing the problem only as it affected her, she had the insight to see that virtually every female who worked in an office faced a similar plight. And on that insight she built a phenomenally successful entrepreneurial company. In November 1984, Carson invested the grand sum of $20 in her new enterprise. Eighteen months later, her sales had grown to an annualized rate of $5 million. Here's how she made that happen:

With her initial $20 investment, Carson bought several packages of plastic fingernails at a five-and-ten for about $3 each. Then she and several family members sat at her kitchen table and lacquered the nails in various colors. Her next step was to test the product: she showed friends, acquaintances, and co-workers how to apply the nails and asked them to try them out. The tests provided a positive response, and Custom Nails, Inc., was born. Carson proceeded with the party plan SDM, moving the business from her kitchen to her garage and then to a 20,000-square-foot plant in Modesto. The company produces nails on a $60,000 mold, which Carson purchased using privately raised financing. One and a half years after launch, Custom Nails hostesses were selling $600 worth of goods per party, and Carson was developing lotions and other hand-care products for her busy reps to sell.

### Other Types of In-Home Marketing

There are some similarities between the party plan SDM and other methods of in-home selling. Insurance policies and mutual funds, for example, are often marketed more or less by this same method. Here are some other products and services you might want to think about in terms of the party plan SDM:

- College guidance counseling
- Hair and skin care for men
- Wellness products
- Home software
- Stress reduction

Regardless of the product or service you choose to market, you'll find that the party plan method becomes physically easier with each technological advance. As of 1986, representatives were able to use the hostess's telephone to enter the orders, deliver the addresses of purchasers, and record the size of their own commissions by phone—all tasks that had to be done in person or by mail not so long ago.

## CELEBRITY-ENDORSED CONSUMER PRODUCT

A celebrity endorsement exists when a well-known person proclaims the virtues of a product or service and when his or her statements are marketed as a testimonial to the high quality of the product or service. Frequently the celebrity is not active in the business, but his or her likeness is used freely. Arthur Murray Dance Studios and Charles Goren's highly successful bridge tour and book business are prime examples. Incidentally, Goren's death has not deterred the revenue growth or profitability of the business he endorsed. The late Nathan Pritikin was relatively active in his successful diet and wellness center in Santa Monica, California, but it continues to thrive in his absence. One of the most successful celebrity-endorsed consumer products companies was the Park-Hines Corporation, launched in 1955 by Roy C. Park, a young advertising executive. Park convinced restaurant critic Duncan Hines to represent the product and do personal appearances. Park-Hines Corporation was subsequently acquired by Procter & Gamble for a substantial sum.

It is the essence of this SDM to conceive of a good product—say, a chain of ballroom-dance instruction studios—and then solicit testimonials from a suitable celebrity—in this instance a dancer, Fred Astaire. Because the product is perceived as bankable, capital can be raised fairly easily, franchises can be sold, then the product can be launched with or without the celebrity's active participation.

Motion picture star Paul Newman stands as a fine example of the entrepreneur-as-giver. For years he had prided himself on the salad dressings he made at his home in Greenwich, Connecticut. Friends who complimented him on his culinary talent often went home with a gift bottle of dressing or a jar of spaghetti sauce. It was these friends who talked Newman into marketing his specialties. Writer A. E. Hotchner signed on as a partner, and Newman's Own, Inc., was born.

Newman and Hotchner began by selling salad dressing and spaghetti sauce through nearby stores in Connecticut. Soon, however, the celebrity endorsement worked its magic. Because Newman is a tremendously famous actor, his name and picture on a new line of food products drew much media attention, and the large supermarket chains began placing orders. Shoppers seemed at first to be buying the Newman's Own merchandise only because of the endorsement. As time went by, however, sales continued to increase, making it clear that people had come back for more, not because of the Newman name but because they really liked the products. Sales in 1986 were running at the $25 million level. The company has a three percent share of the $600 million salad-dressing market, and Newman's Own popcorn accounts for ten percent of its $30 million market.

· And what does an already rich actor do with all of his newly acquired wealth? In the true entrepreneurial spirit, he gives it away. The profits of Newman's Own, Inc., estimated to be $4 million per annum, are sprinkled among 200 different charities, including those dedicated to research into Alzheimer's disease and cancer.

The Newman story seems tailor-made to delight everyone who hears it, right?

Wrong. The competition is grumbling audibly. In its November 4, 1985, issue, *BusinessWeek* quoted a typical complaint about the celebrity's success. Said John S. Craig of Dart-Kraft, Inc., "It makes it hard to compete when people have an opportunity to play by different rules."

And entrepreneurs *do* play by different rules: the rules of entrepreneurship.

## CONSUMER PRODUCT

A large number of consumer products are launched every week. The success rate for this SDM is low, however—mainly because few people take the time to review an item's DEJ factors before putting it on the market. Don't fall into that trap if you choose this solution delivery method. Go back over Chapter 6. Measure your product idea against the DEJ factors and make sure that it has six or more of them. If only five of the DEJ factors apply, your company is almost sure to fail, unless it is a trend catcher such as the Frisbee or the Walkman.

The most frequently absent DEJ factor in new consumer products companies is the big *P*—a large problem in search of a solution. *VisiCalc*, the first spreadsheet software package for the Apple personal computer, and *1-2-3*, the equivalent for the IBM-PC, solve large problems for their users. Most of the other 5,000 software packages launched in 1983 with excessive amounts of venture capital did not solve big problems. Those companies have failed.

Let's say that you have decided to use the consumer product start-up SDM. You have carefully examined the DEJ factors and discovered that you have a majority DEJ business idea. Now you are ready to move forward. Understand at this point that you must execute the launch of your new product very carefully. Here are the steps you must take:

1. Study the market research. Make certain that it indicates a need for the consumer product you have in mind.
2. Find and engage a design and development team who have successfully created a comparable product.
3. Select the marketing channels that will be most appropriate for this particular product: direct mail, catalog or retail sales, franchising, or some other system.
4. Create a PERT chart of the events leading to launch, including a week-by-week or month-by-month time chart (see Chapters 8 and 9).

5. Prepare a business plan by assigning cost values and revenue projections to all items, then explain your strategy to those involved in your company.

6. Produce a prototype of your product.

7. Organize and conduct focus groups of potential purchasers to determine their reaction to your product, its packaging, the price, the appearance, and so forth.

8. Correct or adjust the prototype in accordance with the comments of the potential purchasers; modify your business plan, if necessary.

9. Hire a corporate achiever—an experienced marketing person with a record of success in a related industry—to manage your company.

10. Raise the amount of start-up capital called for in your modified business plan.

11. Begin producing your line of products; put your marketing strategy into operation. (Remember: If your plan calls for a multichannel launch, you may be able to use direct-mail or catalog marketing revenues to finance your marketing to retailers.)

Darby McQuade, who succeeded with a consumer product company, has been an entrepreneur since he was a child. At the age of ten, he was the primary supplier of fishing worms in south central West Virginia. Now he heads Jackalope Pottery, Inc., which he founded in the mid-1970s and which sells more than $4 million in pottery, furniture, and novelty items per annum. "Most people consider doing something, then think up all the reasons why it won't work," says McQuade. "I guess I've never been that way."

All his life, McQuade has thought like an entrepreneur. "I always had some sort of thing going as a kid," he told the *Dallas Morning News* on January 27, 1986. "I sold pop bottles and newspapers, and even pulled a little wagon around selling gourds." By age twenty he was "king of burrito cards" in El Paso. Then he taught school for a while and in his spare time made and sold candles, a part-time job that eventually led him into entrepreneurship on the grand scale.

Soon after going into the candlemaking business on a full-time basis, he placed some of his candles inside attractive Mexican pots. To his surprise, the pots gained more customer attention than the candles did, and his business flourished. He sold it some time later, loaded $2,000 worth of Mexican pottery into his truck, and set out for Sante Fe, New Mexico, where he established Jackalope Pottery, Inc.

McQuade now has a second outlet in Taos, New Mexico, a franchised operation in Fort Worth, and a restaurant in Santa Fe—proof that he still has the courage and insight of which successful entrepreneurs are made.

Another entrepreneur who succeeded with the consumer product SDM is Estee Lauder, whose cosmetics rack up annual sales of $1.25 billion, making Lauder the second largest company in the field (only Avon is bigger). Because it is a privately held company, Estee Lauder and her CEO-son Leonard Lauder can trust their hunches without worrying over quarter-by-quarter profit goals.

In the consumer product business, however, not every hunch will pay off. When one of them fizzles, it's up to the entrepreneur to analyze the problem and then correct it. Lauder's Aramis bombed when it was introduced in 1964. The company recalled the fragrance, repackaged it, and launched it again as a line of men's skin-care products. It now leads the field in men's department-store toiletries.

Another Lauder hunch looked like a failure for a while. It was Clinique, a line of nonallergenic cosmetics that was launched in 1968. For four long years, Clinique lost money—to a total of $20 million. Lauder, believing there was a widespread need for such products, kept it on the market. Today Clinique's sales are over $200 million.

More than 100 years ago, an entrepreneur named Levi Strauss demonstrated the same kind of ingenuity and flexibility that Lauder and McQuade have shown in our time. Strauss earned his living by selling tent canvas to prospectors during the California gold rush. The market for his product was not strong, but instead of giving up, Strauss began to make durable work pants from the tent fabric. He sold the practical and affordable garments to the miners, who called them Levi's, after the man who supplied them.

The Levi Strauss Company became a success primarily because of those work pants, but it continued to look for ways to improve its product. In 1872, a Russian immigrant tailor named Davis discovered a way to keep the pockets of work pants from ripping: he placed a metal rivet at each upper corner. Davis offered the Levi Strauss Company a half-share in the right to sell pants containing these rivets, saying in his letter, "The secrett of them Pents is the Rivits that I put in those Pockets." Strauss's company saw the value of Davis's innovation and began producing the "501 Double X blue denim waist overall, guaranteed to shrink, wrinkle and fade." And Levi's, those most popular of American pants, have remained largely unchanged in the 110 years that have passed since the first riveted jeans were produced.

Estee Lauder, Darby McQuade, and Levi Strauss started out with products that many people wanted, chose the right marketing channels for them, and remained flexible enough to change when they saw a need to do so.

## Creating Awareness of the Need for a Product

A number of entrepreneurs have come up with products that people are not aware they need. The entrepreneurs therefore had to create problem awareness through marketing techniques and then sell their solution to the newly created demand. Listerine mouthwash, which I discussed in Chapter 6, and Rockport ProWalkers, a line of walking shoes, are two fine examples of useful products for which a demand had to be created. Listerine, as I said earlier, became a success after Gene Lasker made the public aware of the problem of halitosis, which the mouthwash solved. Bruce Katz recently took a page from the Listerine book by making people aware of another problem, one that his product could solve.

Katz knew that hundreds of thousands of people were unable, for one reason or another, to jog, play tennis, or do aerobics. He also knew that those people could improve their health by walking for exercise and by wearing his product—sturdy but attractive shoes—while they walked. Katz started out by selling an illustrated book through the stores that carried his shoes. Priced at $8.95, *The Complete Book of Exercise Walking* sold 30,000 copies. Katz also promoted an 11,208-mile cross-country walk by Robert Sweetgall, a fitness missionary. Sweetgall wore Katz's shoes, called Rockport ProWalkers, and gave talks along the way about the health benefits of exercise walking. Another book came out of all of this: *Rockport's Fitness Walking*, which has sold 100,000 copies at $8.95 apiece.

Has Katz's create-awareness-of-the-need-and-then-fill-it plan worked? Rockport's sales were projected to reach $105 million in 1986, up from $7.1 million in 1980. He is now broadening Rockport's line to include all-day shoes for the many women who wear unattractive running shoes to the office and then change into dress shoes. Katz is keeping his company private so as to be able to take calculated risks like creating the need for a product that does not yet exist.

## HIGH TECHNOLOGY

The high-tech SDM has been done supremely well by some computer companies and by biotechnology businesses such as Genentech, Cetus, and Biogen. This is an area in which you, as an entrepreneur, can do a tremendous amount of good—by finding and distributing a cure for a certain disease, let's say, or by discovering a way to make important knowledge available to large numbers of people. However, before you launch a high-tech company, you must have a very clear understanding of this start-up, and you will have to do a thorough analysis of your product to make sure it has all of the DEJ factors.

The initial steps in the high-technology company start-up are similar to those in the consumer product launch:

1. Identify a large problem in search of a solution; determine that the solution is a technological one; determine that the eight DEJ factors are in existence. If one of them is absent—you may face an institutional barrier to entry, such as the FDA—your need for venture capital will increase.

2. Locate a scientific team with demonstrable achievement in the appropriate field, and hire them to design and develop the solution.

3. Create a PERT chart of the events leading to the launch, and make a time schedule.

4. Prepare a business plan by assigning costs to all events; then project costs and subsequent revenues and create a strategy.

5. Produce a prototype of the solution.

6. Beta test your solution with a prospective user and protect it with patents.

7. Debug your solution according to the results of the beta test and modify the business plan accordingly.

8. Hire a corporate achiever from a related industry to manage your company.

9. Raise venture capital—very likely in the dual form of an R&D limited partnership plus private placement with equity—to fund the start-up.

10. Begin production and marketing.

In addition to those ten steps, you may need to make one or more of the following moves to ensure the success of your business:

- Form a scientific advisory board to ensure high standards of quality in production.
- Encourage the formation of users' groups to provide you with continuous marketplace feedback.
- Form a board of directors to help you develop a strong management team and to open industry doors.

The entrepreneurial businesses tabulated in Table 7.1 illustrate the law of the big $P$ (problem), which I explained in Chapter 4 and which, for purposes of review, states that the valuation of a big-$P$ company is equal to the size of the problem rather than to its solution. All ten biotech companies produced substantial financial successes long before they successfully delivered their solutions to large numbers of receivers. This happened because the size of the $P$ they addressed was tremendous.

In the high-technology start-up, the $P$ is crucial, and it must be very large. Let's look at two high-tech businesses, the DeLorean Motor Co., which failed, and Advanced Genetic Systems, which succeeded. What problem did each of those companies set out to solve?

- *DeLorean Motor Co.*   The need for another expensive automobile
- *Advanced Genetic Systems*   The need to find a cure for cancer

In other words, the biotech company aimed at a very big $P$, whereas the DeLorean business set out to solve a $P$ that did not even exist, since the world simply didn't need another high-priced car.

The successful high-tech companies listed in Table 7.1 have skilled and experienced entrepreneurial teams as well, and they offer elegant solutions, but the big $P$—the need to find a cure for cancer or some other terrible disease—is the key to their quick financial success. Big-$P$ companies maintain very high valuations without demonstrating an ability to achieve earnings. In fact, the larger the problem that these companies attempt to solve, the greater their valuations.

*Table 7.1. Biotechnology's Ten Greatest Hits*

| | Avg. Mkt. Price 1986 | | | | Valuation | Profits (Loss) |
|---|---|---|---|---|---|---|
| | High | Low | Avg. | No. Common Shares | ($000) | ($000) |
| 1. Am Gen Corp. | $29\frac{3}{8}$ | $12\frac{3}{8}$ | $20\frac{7}{8}$ | 3,438,000 | $ 71,768 | $ 411 |
| 2. Biogen N. V. | $20\frac{5}{8}$ | $11\frac{1}{2}$ | 16 | 18,590,000 | 297,440 | (20,449) |
| 3. Advanced Genetic Sci. | $6\frac{1}{2}$ | $3\frac{7}{8}$ | $5\frac{1}{4}$ | 12,935,000 | 67,909 | (8,666) |
| 4. Cetus Corp. | $42\frac{1}{2}$ | $22\frac{1}{2}$ | $32\frac{1}{2}$ | 26,022,000 | 845,715 | 1,561 |
| 5. Chiron Corp. | $31\frac{3}{4}$ | $12\frac{1}{8}$ | 22 | 10,703,000 | 235,466 | (5,673) |
| 6. Damon Biotech, Inc. | $10\frac{1}{2}$ | 6 | $8\frac{1}{4}$ | 21,630,000 | 178,448 | (9,517) |
| 7. Genentech, Inc. | $98\frac{3}{4}$ | $32\frac{7}{8}$ | $65\frac{7}{8}$ | 33,020,000 | 2,175,193 | 8,255 |
| 8. Genetic Institute | $33\frac{1}{2}$ | $20\frac{3}{4}$ | $27\frac{1}{8}$ | 11,623,000 | 315,273 | (2,789) |
| 9. Immunex Corp. | $20\frac{1}{4}$ | $12\frac{3}{8}$ | $16\frac{1}{4}$ | 7,393,000 | 120,136 | (3,549) |
| 10. Nova Pharm. | $24\frac{1}{4}$ | $6\frac{7}{8}$ | $15\frac{1}{2}$ | 18,581,000 | 288,005 | (6,874) |
| Average | | | | | $ 459,535 | $( 4,729) |

Source: *Standard & Poor's Stock Guide*, August, 1986.

Just take a look at the problems some of those high-tech companies are going after: hunger, cancer, diabetes. Some of them are working with interferon, a weapon in the fight against cancer. Others set out to improve gene-splicing techniques in the hope that their research may lead to a means of producing insulin within the human body. Still other companies are using genetic engineering to produce seeds that will grow in the sandy soil of the Sudan and someday produce food for the starving people of Africa.

The aggregate market values of the publicly held stocks in one big-P category—cancer—are equal to about $3.5 billion. Genentech alone was valued at $800 million on the first day its stock was publicly traded. Cetus was not Genentechian in size, but its valuation was high nonetheless—about $300 million. And these valuations, remember, are the result of the law of the big $P$ in action.

Ironically, once a big-$P$ company finds the solution to the big problem, begins to deliver that solution, and thus starts to earn large amounts of money, its valuation will rapidly diminish until it evens out as a conventional medium-sized-$P$ company. Why? Because once a $P$ has been solved, it's no longer a big $P$.

## COOKIE CUTTER

"You can't franchise quality," the axiom says. If you have a solution that is best marketed through multiple retail locations, your initial thought may be to sell franchises. After all, it has the attractive benefit of up-front financing from the customer. However, if your product needs to be produced, assembled, or demonstrated by highly skilled people, or if it has an after-sale component, you may have to consider owning and operating the retail outlets yourself and running your business cookie cutter style.

Multiple retail businesses or localized services—for example, Taylor Rental, Renovator's Supply, or Surgicare emergency care centers—offer enormous economies and capital gains potential. When several restaurants sell the same food, dress their employees alike, and decorate their stores in the same way, they can save money by advertising locally, making larger food and supplies purchases, and taking advantage of volume discounts. This way, the profits and rate of return on invested capital can be greater than the rate of return on capital invested in one store. For instance, Church's Fried Chicken has been ranked by *Forbes* magazine as one of the most profitable companies in the country. In five years it earned close to twenty percent per annum on invested capital. Its growth rate exceeded twenty-four percent per annum over the same period.

Modern retail entrepreneurs think in terms of chains, multiples, and cookie cutters, unlike their predecessors, who thought in terms of units—mom-and-pop stores, one-of-a-kind restaurants. Occasionally, a modern cookie-cutter retailer will appear in the midst of a one-of-a-kind family. Take Leslie Wexner, for example.

When Wexner's father, founder of the Limited, a Columbus, Ohio, women's apparel store, went on vacation about fifteen years ago, he asked his son, Leslie, to look after the store for him. When the father returned, the son told him in effect, "I can build this store into a chain, but you have to give me control." The Limited Stores are now over 2,000 strong, and Wexner's wealth exceeds $1 billion built in less than fifteen years.

Another superb example of a cookie-cutter SDM is the retail cookie store. Chocolate chip cookies for $3 per pound would have made my grandmother stop sewing and start baking. As I mentioned earlier, these stores are often located in enclosed malls because the aroma of vanilla is intoxicating. The salespeople at Thom McAnn, Radio Shack, and other shops inside the mall seem suddenly unable to get through the day without five or six cookies.

This SDM is occasionally a component of another start-up method. Frequently, for example, cookie-cutter retail stores are financed with revenues produced by prepaid subscriptions or direct-mail marketing. The founders of Renovator's Supply Company provide an excellent example of this combination of SDMs.

When Claude and Donna Jeanloz began restoring their colonial house in Massachusetts, they found that many of the old-fashioned fixtures they were looking for were no longer easily available. Sheer desperation finally drove them to manufacturers' directories where they hunted down items no one else could supply.

During the four years they spent restoring the Massachusetts home and another house in Canada, they received and answered dozens of letters from people asking where they had found their supplies. Immediately perceiving a widespread problem, the Jeanlozes founded a mail-order business, a clearinghouse for old-fashioned electrical and plumbing fixtures, hardware, and ornaments. Their basic catalog offers necessities for fixing up old houses of any period and in any region. Supplementary catalogs offer specialty products to add finishing details or a touch of nostalgia or whimsy.

As their mail-order business grew, the Jeanlozes moved it into an old garage, which of course they restored. Then, in December 1983, they moved again, this time into a large factory, which also underwent renovation. To generate additional revenues, the Jeanlozes permitted manufacturers to advertise in their catalogs. Sales grew from $34,000 in 1978 to $12 million in 1983.

A stunning cash flow has permitted the Jeanlozes to open a chain of fourteen retail Renovator's Supply stores in New Jersey and New England—a fine example of multiple SDMs.

In March 1984, Renovator's Supply purchased *Aristera*, a catalog of products for left-handed people, and *Country Notebook*, a catalog of country-style home decoration items. Other diversifications include an on-premises blacksmith shop that produces wrought-iron items for the home, and Play for Growth, a line of toys.

Note the clear-headed entrepreneurial insights on which the Jeanlozes based their business. They recognized a widespread problem, saw that they were qualified to solve it, and identified mail order as a form of customer financing.

Another entrepreneur, Tony Harnett, combined clearheadedness with unrelenting determination and, by doing so, achieved success at a time when venture capital was in alarmingly short supply. Harnett, a high school dropout with a good deal of innate business sense, bought a natural food shop in Brookline, Massachusetts, in 1976—in the middle of a deep recession when banks were charging a prime rate of twenty percent. The food store had been faltering badly, so Tony and Susan Harnett were able to acquire it by assuming its liabilities. With hard work, clear entrepreneurial reasoning, good marketing techniques, and sheer resolution, the Harnetts pulled their shop out of the doldrums, made a success of it, and then used the cookie-cutter SDM to build a chain of identical stores. Their Bread 'n' Circus shops were expected to gross $16 million in 1986.

Giorgio Armani combined the cookie-cutter SDM with two other delivery methods—the consumer product start-up and franchising. This combination eventually took his company to the top of the men's and women's apparel field.

Armani's rise to entrepreneurial success followed a classic pathway. Born in Italy of middle-class parents, he attended medical school for three years, dropped out to join the armed services, and then returned to civilian life as a window dresser for an Italian department store called Rinascente. It was in this job that Armani realized he had a gift for design and textiles, and he decided to stay in the apparel field. For seven years in the 1960s, he worked for Cerruti, a men's tailor, where he learned more about the design and manufacture of menswear. He began to work for other manufacturers in 1970 and, with the guidance of business manager Sergio Galeotti, introduced his own designer label in 1974, working out of a two-room office in Milan.

Armani came in at the luxury end of the retail apparel field, introducing bold loose weaves, wrinkled linens, and soft, lightweight wools that suited his independent, physically active audience. When he was firmly established in the luxury market, he began to move downscale. He used the cookie-cutter and franchising SDMs to sell less expensive men's and women's apparel through his Emporio Armani Shops, of which there are eighty in all, sixty-nine of them franchises.

This entrepreneurial progression, as I said, is classic: learning one's trade while working for others, starting out on one's own in a small enterprise, and then hiring managers to grow the company: Armani's annual sales of clothing, royalties, and consulting services now exceeds $100 million.

## CAPITAL EQUIPMENT

The capital equipment SDM requires venture capital in order to get off the ground. A capital-intensive product must be produced, demonstrated to corporate customers, tested, debugged, manufactured, demonstrated again, and finally produced and sold—all of which requires significant amounts of capital. The sales force must then be trained, which will tie up still more capital.

If you wish to become a capital equipment entrepreneur, you must be particularly cognizant of the DEJ factors, because this need for venture capital will dilute your ownership from the beginning. If you lack one or two DEJ factors, your need for capital will increase significantly. Also, your product must solve problems for a large, homogeneous, qualified group of buyers. If it does not do so, your company is likely to fail or to require several rounds of venture capital, thus diluting your ownership even further.

Keep in mind, too, that the rule of 30-30-30 has become the norm among capital equipment start-ups. Here's how it operates: An entrepreneur launches a microprocessor that seems to reduce the cost, increase the speed, and enhance the efficiency of virtually every device it is attached to. As a result, the entrepreneur speaks of a thirty percent improvement in cost, speed, and efficiency. The company's salespeople also speak in terms of the 30-30-30 rule. "This device will allow you to save thirty percent of your departmental costs," they tell their industrial customers. "It will operate thirty percent faster than your current system, and it is thirty percent more efficient." The customer thinks, How can I say no to a product like that?

If a capital equipment company cannot make improvements of at least thirty percent, the product will very likely not sell, since less effective new equipment would not justify its cost in terms of dollars and lost time due to installation. Thus the need for expensive testing, debugging, and retesting before the launch.

I like to use the Rolm Corporation of Santa Clara, California, as an example of a capital equipment company that has succeeded by playing the entrepreneurial game with remarkable expertise. Founded in 1968 by Eugene Richeson, Kenneth Oshman, Walter Lowenstern, and Robert R. Maxfield, the company produces computer-controlled telephone switching systems.

The four founders started out by addressing a large problem: the need for switchboards that were technologically superior to the ones that were then available. In devising their solution, the entrepreneurs kept the 30-30-30 rule in mind all the way: the switching system they developed was thirty percent better, thirty percent faster, and thirty percent cheaper than the one offered by the competition. And they didn't stop improving it even five years later when sales reached $3 million. They kept on developing new features, each of which held up against the 30-30-30 rule. In 1984, Rolm Corporation was acquired by IBM. The price: $1.5 billion.

The story of Rolm's success should give you some idea of the effectiveness of the capital equipment SDM when it is used expertly. Once again, however, analyze those DEJ factors before you make your move, and never forget the 30-30-30 rule. In addition, if you do not cooperate well with people, perhaps you should avoid the capital equipment SDM. In this SDM, you will need a large group of venture capitalists to fuel your launch.

## TOLLGATE

Some of the most lucrative companies in America are those that extract a fee from people who wish to enter a certain market or area—in the manner of a tollgate owner who charges those who wish to use a certain highway. The government is of course the primary user of this SDM. It has erected a number of tollgates to prevent people from entering certain professions, doing certain things, or going to certain places without first paying a toll—proving that the government knows a good deal when it sees one.

When governments put up too many tollgates in too many markets, however, they snuff the life out of the economy and destroy profits.

France experienced this problem after the Mitterrand administration nationalized its major corporations. Eventually, Mitterrand had to backpedal by selling some of the tollgates to entrepreneurs through facilities management contracts.

The U.S. government, though it has not gone as far as that, does control a good number of tollgates. How many can you think of in addition to the following?

- Literal tollgates on U.S. highways
- Drivers' licenses
- Food and Drug Administration
- Certification tests for licenses in teaching, medicine, cosmetology, and other professions.
- Passport and customs fees, and other tollgates through which international travelers must pass

In the area of private enterprise, the object of the tollgate is to allow an entrepreneur to extract a fee from those who wish to come into the market whose gateway he or she controls, gain an advantage that the entrepreneur can provide, or receive certain kinds of information that can come only through the entrepreneur. This need for a certain commodity becomes the justification for erecting the tollgate. Mario Puzo's novel, *The Godfather,* points out how protection became the justification for the tollgate put in place in many markets by one group of immigrant entrepreneurs. (Many of those protection tollgate entrepreneurs have not enjoyed long lives, however. There seems to be a health risk associated with this form of tollgate.)

Exclusivity, or snob appeal, is frequently just as effective a justification for a tollgate as the need for protection is. In fact, real estate developers have used a combination of the two to sell high-priced condominiums and houses in private communities. They justify the expense by appealing to the buyers' desire for exclusivity and by promising the protection of twenty-four-hour guard service and television-camera surveillance of all those who dare to approach the tollgate. Fear has always served as an inducement to those who provide protection, but the honest entrepreneur will take care not to create unnecessary fear with promises of fortresslike security.

Eustis Paine has established a tollgate company that makes life easier for all concerned and earns a profit for the toll collector at the same time. By doing this, he has managed to revolutionize the wine industry, the largest single employer in his adopted country France.

Paine is a computer buff who spent five years learning the wine business as a ship's provisioner in the U.S. Virgin Islands. With his extraordinary entrepreneurial vision, he took a hard look at the wine industry and saw a 300-year-old business cloaked in mystery, snobbism, secrecy, and unnecessary mercantile baggage. He saw a way of trimming that industry down and thereby making it more manageable and more profitable for wine makers and distributors.

Paine learned that no less than seven steps were required to move a bottle of Bordeaux from the château where it was made to the consumer in the United States. Every one of those movements added a markup to the wine. The seven steps were as follows:

1. The château itself, which serves as the bottler for one of the wine-making regions of France
2. The *negociant,* a French distributor of wines
3. The freight forwarder
4. The American importer
5. The American wholesaler
6. The retailer who sells the wine in the United States
7. The American consumer who buys the wine

Because of this complicated chain of handlers, a bottle of wine that cost about 65 cents to produce would be sold to the American consumer for about $8.50. In a restaurant it would cost about $17.00! 

Paine also knew that wine prices varied in an irrational manner, sometimes according to the size of a château's production, the quality of the wine as determined by so-called wine experts, and the marketing skill of various distributors along the complicated road that led from wine maker to consumer.

By establishing a tollgate near the beginning of that road, Paine succeeded in eliminating some of the expensive stopovers that each bottle of wine was forced to make. First, he formed Winex, Ltd., in Libourne, France, in 1984. His next step was to create a software program that would enable wine purchasers from other nations to gain immediate access to information about available stock. Then he persuaded the French châteaus to put information about their wines into Winex's computer: name, address, telephone number, available quantities of wine according to year of production, quality, delivery time, and price. Unsurprisingly, the châteaus were reluctant at first to provide price information, but they have now begun to see the value of Paine's tollgate: when people buy direct from the châteaus through Winex, the wine makers secure a much greater share of the profit.

When the Winex computer contained sufficient information, Paine got in touch with the largest wine importers in the five major wine-consuming nations: the United States, West Germany, the United Kingdom, Italy, and France itself. He offered them computer terminals on a rental basis, along with connect time to the Winex data bank. By using the Winex service, these people trace their orders better, save mountains of paperwork, and speed up their deliveries. The châteaus, in turn, receive faster payment and a larger share of the profits.

Winex's typical customer stays connected to the data bank for more than one hour each day, which translates into a great many quarters being fed into Paine's electronic tollgate. As Winex began its second year of operation, its revenues were running in excess of $1 million per annum.

Information often serves as a reason to exact tolls from people—all kinds of information, not just data about wine. Remember the shouts of scorecard vendors as you enter a stadium: "You can't tell the players without a scorecard!"

A scorecard of sorts acts as a means of controlling the flow of information in many markets. Here are three of them. Can you think of others?

1. Executive search firms
2. Travel agencies
3. Directories such as *TV Guide, Guide Michelin,* and the *Racing Form*

In a rapidly changing world the need for up-to-date information has become greater than ever before, and the price of that updated information has increased accordingly. So far, however, the methods of delivery have remained pretty much the same—books, newsletters, magazines, radio and TV programs, and now videocassettes. If you are still trying to come up with an entrepreneurial idea, keep in mind that the older forms of delivering information may soon be adapted for distribution through computer networks. The *Thomas Register of Manufacturers,* for example, will certainly be available through such networks someday, or it will be replaced by one that is. The same is true for directories of actors, pharmaceuticals, performers, electronic parts, and legal services. Here are three more ideas for tollgate companies:

- Medical records on a chip embedded in a credit card
- A medical encyclopedia transmitted through a computer network
- An international shopping service via cable TV

## NEWSLETTER-SEMINAR

The newsletter-seminar SDM is used when the entrepreneur has the capacity to provide information that large numbers of people need. This can be the simplest possible method of delivering a solution—as when a firearms expert publishes a monthly newsletter on guns and holds an annual seminar for gun enthusiasts. Or it can evolve into a complex network of information services like International Data Group, Inc., founded by Patrick J. McGovern, which publishes sixty-two magazines and newspapers serving a wide spectrum of readers (see Chapter 6).

Let's take a look at the ways in which a successful entrepreneur could deliver helpful information (S) to a market in which information is scarce or nonexistent (P).

Realize, first of all, that the newsletter-seminar SDM is best used when no solution has yet been fully developed and when the people who have the problem are not yet ready to pay for its solution or are not yet aware of the extent to which the problem exists. At this point—the earlier the better—the entrepreneur steps in and offers a solution in the form of a conference or a newsletter that provides a forum for the exchange of information.

Suppose you are this entrepreneur and you've decided to begin by publishing a newsletter. In it you will provide information about the problem you have formulated. At the same time, you will be generating awareness of your understanding of this problem, thus establishing yourself as an authority in your field. Prepaid subscriptions to your newsletter will provide you with a steady cash flow. If the problem is sufficiently large, advertisers who wish to address your readers will buy space in the newsletter, thus creating a second source of revenue. (*Ms.* magazine, which addresses the issue of equality for women, was launched in this manner.)

You may decide at a fairly early point to establish still another source of revenues by organizing a conference or a series of seminars at which members of your audience can get together, exchange ideas with one another, and listen to the solutions that have been developed by you and by other experts in the field.

Eventually your newsletter-seminar business will lead you into a fourth and a fifth revenue-generating operation—consulting, perhaps, and/or facilities management. Carefully nurtured and cultivated, the growth of your company's market will assume the shape of a pyramid: one or two receivers at the top will become ten or twenty contracts, which in turn will lead to fifty or seventy-five more receivers, and so on until the market pyramid has a large, strong base of customers. (See Figure 7.1.)

## The Pyramid Launch

I often use as an example the story of an entrepreneur who chose the newsletter-seminar SDM and embarked on a pyramid launch. Because it illustrates all aspects of the launch, I think that story bears repeating here:

> The human resources officer in a large corporation, in the course of her work, became aware of a problem that she termed "relocation stress." The problem affected middle managers who were transferred often from one corporate branch to another. As a result of the frequent moves, the managers, their spouses, and their children could not form lasting friendships and had no time to make themselves a part of a community. Children's schoolwork slipped badly and their social development suffered. Marriages cracked under the strain of frequent relocation.
>
> Seeing her co-workers being torn apart emotionally by this relocation stress, the human resources officer suggested to her supervisor that families receive counseling before they were transferred.
>
> Her boss liked the idea and permitted the human resources officer to interview employees and families who had been asked to relocate. Her purpose was to devise a means of solving the problem of relocation stress. As time passed, she became experienced in solving this problem and made senior management more sensitive to its existence.
>
> Up to this point, the human resources officer had been generally satisfied with her job. Now, however, her supervisor left the corporation, and the new boss abruptly ended her counseling activities. His reason, he explained, was that "any employee who bucks at the suggestion of relocation is not a team player and ought to be canned."
>
> The human resources officer went through the dissatisfaction–insight–energy progression that turns mild-mannered Clark Kent into Superman.

**Figure 7.1.** The growth of a company's market will assume the shape of a pyramid.

Then she walked into the new boss's office and resigned, intending to become a relocation stress consultant.

The newly fledged entrepreneur sketched a pyramid such as the one in Figure 7.1 to give herself an idea of the potential size of her market. Her plan was to begin with 2,000 human resources officers who worked for corporations known to relocate their managers with some frequency. She meant to educate them about the problem of relocation stress through the newsletter-seminar SDM, with the goal of obtaining short-term consulting contracts and the ultimate aim of turning one or more of the corporations into long-term contract clients. Let's take a close look at the way in which this entrepreneur proceeded.

She began by publishing a newsletter, which would serve as a problem-finding and problem-formulating tool and as a device to heighten awareness of the $P$ to which she wished to offer an $S$.

(Let me digress from this story long enough to say that every industry should have a newsletter. If you wish to publish one, however, you must be ready when that industry is born—or else you must create the industry yourself. Otherwise you'll be too late, for someone else will have jumped in ahead of you. For example, are you thinking of disseminating information about antique eyewash cups? Sorry. You're already too late. The eyewash cup collectors' newsletter has been around for years.)

The relocation stress entrepreneur offered her newsletter to the 2,000 human resources officers on a prepaid subscription basis, ten issues for $120. Four hundred of the officers subscribed, so the entrepreneur now had $48,000 in launch capital. It is possible to attract advertisers for a newsletter, but this particular newsletter did not immediately suggest any good ideas for ads.

Two or three months of publishing went by. The entrepreneur reported on the subject of relocation stress from every vantage point imaginable: the human angle, the legal angle, the moral angle, and so forth. In the fourth month, believing that some of her subscribers were ready to meet to discuss the issue, she announced a seminar. For a $500 fee, the human resources officers were invited to meet in Chicago for two days of panel discussions and lectures by psychologists and psychiatrists. The entrepreneur received checks from seventy-five human resources officers, totaling $37,500. She spent $10,000 to arrange a first-class seminar: a well-organized, varied program, top-notch speakers, excellent food, a pleasant ambiance, and comfortable accommodations—paid for by the attendees—in a safe, interesting, and easily accessible neighborhood. She later earned back that $10,000 by selling tapes of the seminar sessions for $75 each.

As a result of the seminar, the officers gained a better understanding of the extent of the relocation stress problem, and the entrepreneur gained seventy-five valuable corporate contacts. She offered each attendee a one-day consultation session for $1,000. Twenty corporations signed one-day contracts, for further revenues of $20,000, and the entrepreneur was now increasing the size of the pyramid's base.

As a result of the twenty one-day consulting sessions, she won two performance contracts. She would counsel all families that had been asked to relocate and would advise the corporation as to whether those families were capable of handling the stress or whether they should not yet be moved.

The contracts were worth $25,000 each plus expenses, and each contract had a duration of one year. Thus after the first twelve months of operation, the entrepreneur had generated more than $145,000 in revenues in the kind of pyramid launch illustrated in Figure 7.1.

By the way, the relocation stress launch story is fictional. You can go out and do it yourself.

### Additional Revenue Sources

Now that you've seen an example of a newsletter-seminar launch, let's get back to those additional revenue-generating sources I mentioned a moment ago. Our relocation stress expert established three sources of revenue: newsletter, conference, and consultation. That's an impressive record, to be sure, but many more revenue sources could be put into operation.

Let's say that you have chosen the newsletter-seminar SDM as the means of delivering your solution (information) to the problem you have formulated (a widespread need for the information you can provide). You start by launching a service magazine in your field, thus generating two revenue sources: prepaid subscriptions and advertisements. But if you truly have an entrepreneur's heart, you don't stop there. You ask yourself what other sources of revenue remain to be explored. Here are some of the answers you might come up with:

- Mailing list rentals
- Offering consumer products manufactured by others to subscribers via direct mail
- Seminars and symposia
- Consulting services, reports about the industry, market research studies of the subscribers
- Videocassettes and audiocassettes of feature articles

- Television documentaries and computer software packages of feature articles
- Sale of feature articles to publishers of small-town Sunday newspaper supplements and to foreign magazine and newspaper publishers
- Publication of feature articles in book form
- Publication of directories containing information about key members of the industry
- Publication of reference guides containing valuable articles from other magazines that are relevant to the industry and also offering news of industry-related events
- Sale of calendars, diaries, and related items
- Sale of T-shirts, sweat shirts, and tote bags
- Establishment of tours, camps, and weekend conferences

With each of these sub-SDMs generating cash flow, much of it prepaid, your newsletter-seminar entrepreneurial company will be turning a profit. There is little wonder that our country has such a large number of information industry megabuck entrepreneurs. Many of them have built companies with more than twenty revenue sources.

One of the most imaginative information industry entrepreneurs is Patrick J. McGovern, whom I discussed in Chapter 6 and who was one of the first people to recognize the need for information in the fledgling computer industry. The original purpose of his company was to provide market research to computer vendors, but in true entrepreneurial style, McGovern did not stop there. International Data Group, Inc., as I have already pointed out, now puts out a host of publications, including its flagship magazine, *Computerworld*, which brings in $42 million per annum in advertising alone.

Here are just a few of the other entrepreneurs who have built information companies with multiple revenue sources after starting with the newsletter-seminar SDM:

- Richard Ekstract, founder of Viare Publishing Corp., provides information about the home video market.
- T. George Harris provides data about good health; his flagship publication is *American Health*.
- Gloria Steinem founded *Ms.* magazine to address the problems faced by women in today's world.
- Rupert Murdoch used leveraged buy-outs to acquire numerous magazines, newspapers, and television stations.

These are only four examples from among the hundreds of successful entrepreneurs who have built diversified companies that provide information to those who need it. If you are interested in joining these people, you will first identify a problem that can be solved by the newsletter-seminar SDM. A few such problems come immediately to mind:

- The need for information about entrepreneurship
- The lack of published data about the rodeo industry
- The problem of stress
- The difficulties faced by stepfamilies

## FRANCHISE ON OPA

Instead of investing in capital equipment or bricks and mortar to start a new business, you might be able to obtain a franchise on OPA (other people's assets). This SDM involves delivering your solution by means of an object that someone else already owns.

ActMedia, for example, was started in 1976 by Bruce Failing and his family as an in-store media company. The Failings convinced large consumer products companies of the effectiveness of placing their ads at the point of purchase: on shopping carts. The entrepreneurs tested the idea in several large supermarkets and calculated the results. Product sales increased dramatically in stores where shopping carts carried advertisements. With very little investment at the front end, ActMedia's market value exceeded $150 million in nine years. The Failings' entrepreneurial company was basically a franchise on the OPA of the supermarkets.

Many other businesses have built franchises on OPA. They include:

- A. C. Nielsen & Company whose product is records of television viewing and whose OPA is other people's TV sets
- Dow Jones & Company where the solution is financial information and the OPA is the invested capital of U.S. industry
- Movie producers whose product is motion pictures, delivered through the OPA of theaters and TV sets
- Radar detector manufacturers, who use two different OPAs: the vehicles owned by drivers and the radar equipment owned by police departments

Managers who have been at their jobs for a long time frequently overlook OPAs that have enormous value. Sometimes an imaginative entrepreneur can walk into their company, take a fresh look around, and seize an asset that the management team has been unaware of for years.

The management of Arm & Hammer Corporation in 1970 called in marketing consultant Gerald Schoenfeld to resuscitate sales of its oldest product, baking soda. Schoenfeld studied the product's history and noticed a 125-year-old ad that said baking soda could be used to clean iceboxes and sweeten cutting boards. Schoenfeld noted that people do not clean their refrigerators with great frequency, so he revised the ad to suggest placing an open box of baking soda inside the refrigerator and freezer to absorb food odors. One year later, 33 million refrigerators contained a box of Arm & Hammer baking soda. Schoenfeld had seen in all those refrigerators an OPA that had escaped everyone else.

William Steinberg is a businessman with a good eye for OPA. His company, Tradewell Industries, Inc., buys failed product lines from consumer products manufacturers and then sells them through distribution channels the original company overlooked. One of the OPAs he acquired was an unsuccessful cat litter. What does one do with kitty litter that isn't any good? Steinberg sold it to horse stables, which used it in place of sawdust.

John Werner Kluge is another entrepreneur who is quick to recognize the value of OPA. Born in Chemnitz, Germany, Kluge came to the United States as a child with his parents, who settled in Detroit. After having established a successful food brokering business, he joined with a group of friends in the purchase of a controlling interest in Metropolitan Broadcasting, a company that owned television stations in Washington, D.C. and New York City. After being renamed Metromedia, the company acquired five additional TV stations, fifteen radio stations, and an advertising company. It also bought the Harlem Globetrotters and the Ice Capades.

Kluge's genius, however, lay in his ability to see straight through a broadcasting company to the profits—in other words, the OPA—that were hidden deep inside its balance sheet. He knew that such items as amortization, depreciation, and interest payments could obscure the assets of the company and even cause the books to show a loss. By regarding such noncash expenses as OPA, Kluge was able to fund a number of acquisitions that brought Metromedia $2 billion in 1986, the year he sold the company to Rupert Murdoch.

One series of acquisitions came about in 1982 when Kluge heard that the FCC planned to distribute cellular licenses to telephone companies and independent businesses. Within two months, Metromedia had spent $180 million to purchase six paging-beeper companies, all of which had applied for cellular licenses from the FCC. A bit later on, Kluge picked up two more similar companies, making Metromedia the leader in paging devices. It also has cellular telephone companies in six large American cities. These businesses should bring Kluge another billion some time in the near future—a second fortune built on OPA.

Another American entrepreneur who recognized the value of OPA was Oakleigh B. Thorne, who founded Commerce Clearing House, Inc., more than thirty years ago. CCH, a suburban Chicago company, is a franchise on other people's assets. In this instance, the assets are changes in the laws of the United States. CCH gathers information about legislation—at no cost, of course, since such changes are a matter of public record and are thus available to anyone who can take the time to look them up. CCH prints up the information on loose-leaf pages, pops them into notebooks, and charges in advance to mail them to people who need this kind of information. Some 50,000 lawyers, legislators, political scientists, law professors, and others pay $1,075 to receive the CCH reports for one year.

The profit margins for a franchise on OPA such as CCH's are extraordinary. The company earned $45 million after taxes in 1985 on revenues of $470 million, and it had over $100 million in cash on hand. Although two other companies, Prentice-Hall and Research Institute, have now entered the field, CCH still holds on to fifty-six percent of the market.

Successful entrepreneurs use one or more of these twelve solution delivery methods, or SDMs, to make their products and services accessible to receivers. As an aspiring entrepreneur, you should examine them carefully and then select the one that best suits your business idea. To understand the importance of choosing the right SDM, think of the marketplace as a dense forest, thick with underbrush, and of the SDMs as paths through that forest, leading to the customers you wish to reach. If you choose the right path, you will be able to go directly from your starting point to the marketplace. If you choose the wrong one, you could get lost in the jungle for months, or forever. Study each path carefully before you set out to deliver your solution. Choose the one that offers the most direct and obstacle-free route to your receivers.

If you find yourself wandering away from the SDM you have so carefully chosen, remind yourself that many entrepreneurial companies have failed miserably simply because they chose the wrong solution delivery method. If you need an example, think of the entrepreneurial graveyard now filled with the remains of computer software companies that ignored catalog marketing (prepaid subscription), celebrity endorsement, and franchise on OPA (licensing the name of an educational publisher) and plunged forward pigheadedly with a consumer product start-up. Recall also the many fast-food retailers who failed to make the cut because they ignored the franchising SDM. There are probably several abandoned fast-food locations in your hometown.

Many creative entrepreneurs have demonstrated an ability to discover and use numerous subsets of SDMs to generate as many as twenty or even thirty separate and distinct channels to consumers and an equal number of sources of revenue for their companies. Earlier in this chapter, in discussing the newsletter-seminar SDM, I showed you how a simple newsletter could grow and expand into a multiple-SDM company that might have sold consumer products (T-shirts and tote bags) as well as information.

As your entrepreneurial company develops, keep looking for ways to utilize other SDMs or other aspects of your original solution delivery method.

# 8

## *Entrepreneurial Solutions To Twenty-five of Today's Problems*

To demonstrate that entrepreneurship really is a discipline that can be taught, you should now be able to put your understanding of the laws and fundamentals of the process to work by solving some of society's problems.

In this chapter I will first list twenty-five of the problems people face in today's world—what I call big *P*'s. Then I'll start you out on the process of solving them entrepreneurially. I'll do this by guiding you through two of the twelve steps in the entrepreneurial process: problem formulation and solution development. For some of these big-*P* solutions I'll give you a PERT chart, which is a schematic diagram of your company's launch— PERT stands for program evaluation and review tool. Developed by the Rand Corporation in the early 1960s, the chart was designed to help the businessperson schedule the many and varied steps that lead toward an ultimate goal—in this case, the launch. This tool will be explained in greater detail in the Drunk Driving section of this chapter.

Here are the twenty-five serious problems in search of solutions:

1. The high crime rate among urban teenage boys
2. Incompetent government officials

3. Drunk driving
4. Easy availability of cocaine and heroin
5. Terrorism
6. Unemployment in older industries
7. Stepparenting
8. Excessive cost and ineffectiveness of the U.S. penal system
9. High cost of legal aid
10. Difficulty of commuting to work
11. Stress
12. Waste management
13. Misuse of alcohol and drugs by teenagers
14. High cost of college tuition
15. Male sexual impotence
16. Roaches
17. Potholes
18. Care of the aged
19. Graffiti
20. Bankrupt U.S. farm system
21. Low reading scores
22. Lack of retail stores in inner cities
23. High cost of Social Security
24. Lack of affordable high-quality day care
25. Cancer research

Now let's look at these items in detail. I'll formulate a problem, devise one possible solution, then choose and explain the SDMs. As you work your way through these exercises, flex your newly acquired entrepreneurial muscles by elaborating on the outlines I provide. Also keep in mind that you have complete freedom to reject the solution I offer and devise one of your own—provided you are certain it will work equally as well as or better than the one I suggest.

## HIGH CRIME RATE AMONG URBAN TEENAGE BOYS

### Problem Formulation

Teenage boys, often operating in gangs, have turned some urban neighborhoods into combat zones. Together or individually they commit crimes ranging from vandalism and petty larceny to murder, rape, and arson. Robbery has, in effect, become the "profession" of many boys who have lived their entire lives in poverty.

## Solution Development

You could solve this problem by providing a legal source of income for urban teenagers. Keeping in mind that many poor city residents earned a living in the past through entrepreneurial activities—fruit and vegetable stands, for example—you could work toward channeling the energy of these teenagers into hundreds of small businesses. As the businesses began to generate income, the teenagers' need, or desire, to commit crimes would diminish.

## Solution Delivery Method

This entrepreneurial opportunity requires *celebrity endorsement*. Perhaps a dozen celebrities, self-made men and women who grew up in poor neighborhoods, would be willing to sponsor an urban small business generator. The entrepreneurial company, let's call it My Marketplace, Inc. (MMI), would collect, at no charge to itself, excess inventories from corporations in the city. These goods would be picked up by vans each evening and driven to central breakdown warehouses, where they would be divided according to the category—food, clothing, household goods, office equipment, automotive equipment, carpentry tools—among the various small businesses owned by the teenagers.

Service businesses would donate instructors in accounting, advertising, and banking to assist the young business owners. Financial institutions would donate the initial capital to MMI to pay for the vans and labor, and MMI would lend each small business $10,000 to begin operations. The city would provide condemned buildings under long-term leases to MMI for release to the small businesses at affordable rents.

Three SDMs are used in the MMI concept:

1. *Facilities Management.* MMI agrees to manage the crime-prevention facility for the city and receives payment in advance and on an ongoing basis in the form of goods, services, and capital.
2. *Celebrity Endorsement.* Some socially concerned athletes, financiers, entertainers, and executives would volunteer to take a visible, active, and concerned role.
3. *Franchise on OPA.* MMI "takes from the rich" its excess food, clothing, and other goods and services, and gives to the poor an opportunity

to get into business for themselves, without having to generate large amounts of capital to produce the food, clothing, or whatever.

## INCOMPETENT GOVERNMENT OFFICIALS

### Problem Formulation

Most Americans claim to be generally displeased with the performance of their elected officials. In the next election, they turn them out of office and put others in their place. But voting seems to be an activity that people perform with overwhelming incompetence, and so each election produces another wave of unsatisfactory officials. We need to break this cycle of incompetent voting, which produces waste, inflation, and a massive, top-heavy bureaucracy.

### Solution Development

Consumers tend to read information about products immediately before purchasing them. For example, they will read point-of-purchase display materials. Politicians may be considered a type of consumer product, and data about their performance can be gathered, stored, and presented in various forms.

### Solution Delivery Method

An entrepreneur forms a company on the state level, to begin with, to gather political voting records and do probability analyses of politicians' voting patterns. The company then predicts the way certain politicians will vote on specific issues. If these predictions have a better than seventy-five percent degree of accuracy, the company has a salable service: a system that will help people decide whom they wish to vote for.

This system could be marketed using one or more of the following SDMs:

1. *Prepaid subscriptions* to frequently updated electronic data banks, specially tailored for the news media.
2. *Newsletter-seminar* directed at politically aware individuals and groups who wish to receive information regularly.
3. *Tollgate* at which politicians must pay a fee in order to be considered for inclusion in the information service—much as consumer electronics products manufacturers pay Underwriters Laboratories to test their products before shipping them to retailers.

## DRUNK DRIVING

### Problem Formulation

An estimated 23,500 lives are lost each year in the United States as a result of drunk driving. There is no apparent means of inducing all drivers to refrain from drinking, although recent changes in drinking-age laws and pressure from citizens' groups have made some progress in that direction.

### Solution Development

It is technically possible to design and produce an electronic alcohol sensor that would make drunk driving virtually impossible. This device, when implanted on the dashboard or steering wheel of a car, would detect the presence of a specified amount of alcohol in the driver's breath and would automatically lock the vehicle's ignition. The microchip in this sensor would probably cost less than $5 to manufacture in large quantities.

### Solution Delivery Method

The entrepreneurial company would conduct clinical tests and trials to develop sufficient "Hey, it really works" data. Perhaps a community where drunk driving is a particular problem would be willing to put the sensors in all cars of citizens arrested for driving while intoxicated in order to generate Beta-test data. Or a car manufacturer might conduct its own test by simply installing the sensors on all new cars as part of a socially concerned marketing campaign. An entrepreneurial car company, such as Honda, would be a more likely candidate, since entrepreneurial companies are problem solvers by nature. Companies that make small components for oligopolistic industries are like mice scrambling for cover among an army of elephants. For example, can you name the inventor of windshield wipers? Thus the manufacturer of the alcohol sensor chip should consider a fairly early merger into a company that produces numerous components for car and truck manufacturers.

### One Entrepreneur's Solution

Kip Fuller, a young Denver entrepreneur, has developed a different kind of solution to the drunk driving problem, one that is voluntary rather than mandatory. He is marketing a device called the Guardian Interlock, a breath-analyzing instrument that is placed on the dashboard of a vehicle.

Before starting the car, a driver blows into the interlock, which measures the alcohol content of his or her breath. A green light will come on after a few seconds if the person is capable of driving safely, and the ignition will be activated. If a yellow light appears, the driver is warned that he or she is approaching the danger limit but is still able to drive with care. Again, the ignition is activated. A red light, however, tells the person not to drive and at the same time prevents him or her from starting the car.

Fuller's product retails for $295 and went on the market in 1986. Customers include drivers who are concerned about their own lives and parents who worry about their children who drive.

The PERT chart that follows is designed to take the manufacturer of an alcohol sensor through the launch process one step at a time. Note that the chart moves through time (plotted in months from left to right), taking into consideration the various entrepreneurial areas (from top to bottom), including finances, the product, plant and equipment, people, and administration. As you proceed through the steps in the PERT, assign a cost to each action.

## EASY AVAILABILITY OF COCAINE AND HEROIN

### Problem Formulation

Cocaine has become the drug of the middle class, the social drug. To take cocaine is to make a statement: "I have enough money to afford it."

Close to 30 million Americans are believed to have experimented with the drug. Some sources say that fifty percent of all teenagers have tried cocaine at least once.

Medical opinions on the effects of long-term cocaine usage are fairly unanimous: it can cause brain damage and, as we know from the Len Bias case, death. Graduates of cocaine and its liquid form, crack, frequently move on to heroin. This is a deadly drug that is highly addictive and the cause of a great deal of crime.

Both drugs are easily available, not only in large U.S. cities, but in small towns and rural areas as well. Putting a stop to this ease of access is a problem of extreme importance.

### Solution Development

The government's crackdown on illegal imports of the raw materials that find their way into cocaine and heroin factories has been more hopeful than helpful. Voluntary efforts have had the positive effect of making a

PERT: *Alcohol Sensor*

| Months: | 1 | 2 | 3 | 4 | 5 |
|---|---|---|---|---|---|
| Finances: | Meet with family, friends; begin writing business plan | Raise funds from family and friends | Apply to foundations, National Science Foundation; staff defers wages | Complete, submit business plan to banks, SBA, BDC, IDA | Meet with local banks, SBA, BDC, IDA |
| Product: | | | Begin project engineering and development (PED)—research intensive | Additional PED | Additional PED—development intensive |
| Plant and equipment: | Use dining room table; look for high-technology business incubator | Look for high-technology business incubator | Apply to incubator; get costs on microchip equipment | Move into incubator; rent additional equipment | Modify equipment |
| People: | Interview electrical engineers, chemical technicians; interview legal consultants | Additional interviews; hire legal consultant | Hire electrical engineers, chemical technicians | Incubator provides secretarial services, board of advisors | Local graduate students assist in bookkeeping and laboratory |
| Administration: | Incorporate; design logo; stationery | Determine liabilities of microchip sensor malfunctions | Obtain grant application: consult Federal Code of Regulations | Hold initial board meeting | Establish bookkeeping procedures |
| Marketing: | | | | | |

*PERT: Alcohol Sensor* (Continued)

| Months: | 6 | 7 | 8 | 9 | 10 |
|---|---|---|---|---|---|
| Finances: | Take out small loan; modify, submit business plan to incubator seed fund, venture capitalists | Meet with venture capitalists; proceed with due diligence; modify, submit business plan to entrepreneurial car cos. (e.g., Honda) | Additional due diligence with venture capitalists; meet with corporate planning officers; proceed with due diligence | Additional due diligence with venture capitalists; corporate planning officers | Structure joint venture—license marketing rights with buyout option; apply for UDAG |
| Product: | Additional PED; complete prototype design | Additional PED; build prototype; conduct alpha test | Debug prototype; prepare manufacturing feasibility study | Additional debugging; decide on manufacturing plan | Microchip debugged; alpha tests complete |
| Plant and equipment: | Get costs on car equipment | Rig microchip sensor to car starter | Meet with equipment suppliers | Negotiate with suppliers; decide on plant location—industrial parks | Contract with second source suppliers; apply to industrial park |
| People: | Interview legal, manufacturing consultant | Hire legal, manufacturing consultant | Interview chief administrative officer | Additional interviews; interview plant manager | Hire chief administrative officer; additional interviews |
| Administration: | File patent disclosure | File patent; register trademark; hold second board meeting | | Key man insurance; apply to HUD; establish employee stock option plan | Amend patent if necessary; register trademark; PERT chart plant operations, scheduling |
| Marketing: | Write mission sheet, "welcome to our company" | Seek endorsements from MADD, etc. | | | |

| Months: | 11 | 12 | 13 | 14 | 15-17 | 18 |
|---|---|---|---|---|---|---|
| Finances: | Close deal; raise venture capital | Car company finances capital equipment | Materials suppliers finance work-in-process | Car co. finances finished goods with advanced payments | | |
| Product: | Car company organizes community beta test | | Begin small-scale beta tests, debugging; begin continuous process | Additional beta tests; debug continuous process | Additional beta tests; debugging | Complete beta tests, debugging |
| Plant and equipment: | Rent, lay out plant with adjoining office | Modify plant; lease equipment; car co. engineers assist with tooling and assembly | Assemble continuous process equipment | Modify equipment | | Upgrade automated equipment to meet car company demands |
| People: | Hire plant manager, secretary, bookkeeper; interview foreman; seek board of directors | Hire foreman, operators; interview purchasing, receiving managers | Hire purchasing, receiving managers interview shipping clerk, marketing consultant | Form board of directors; hire shipping clerk, marketing consultant | Initial board meeting | Schedule new production requirements |
| Administration: | Get fire, group, health, workers' compensation insurance | Establish purchasing, receiving, inventory management system; first financial report to shareholders | Establish quality control system; transportation, shipping logistics | | | |
| Marketing: | Media announcement | | Attend community meetings with car company representatives and legal consultant | Attend additional community meetings; investigate new products, markets | Attend periodic community meetings with car company representatives | Car company markets product worldwide |

larger number of teenagers aware of the dangers of drug use, but they have been top-down attempts, which at best produce results only in the long term.

### Solution Delivery Method

The best long-term solution I've seen was suggested by John D. MacDonald in his novel, *The Lonely Silver Rain*. According to MacDonald, the government would immediately change the color of paper money worth $20 or more. It might, for example, print red $100 bills, blue $50 bills, and purple $20 bills. It would require all citizens to go to their banks within thirty days, turn in their old bills, and receive the new, colored currency. Green paper money would immediately become worthless.

Drug dealers would be caught between a rock and a hard place. If they showed up with tens of thousands of dollars in cash, they would be questioned as to its source. If they did not exchange their money, they would be too broke to purchase more drugs. Drug traffic would stop until new dealers took over, using the new colorful money. They would live with monumental uncertainty as to when the money would change color again. This level of risk would drive half the drug dealers out of business. The remainder would cease activities at the next change of color.

A possible entrepreneurial opportunity is to become the company that creates the colored paper money. An entrepreneur could formulate the problem in depth, perhaps by interviewing officials in the Drug Enforcement Agency—particularly with regard to the flow of money—measure the effect of the colored money exchange solution, PERT chart it, define the cost to the government, to banks, and to innocent people, then begin an intense lobbying campaign in Washington to force through the plan.

Perhaps you have already detected a flaw in this plan: the delivery method is not one of the twelve classic SDMs and is therefore doomed to failure from the outset. The problem is that it relies on an exogenous variable that is beyond the entrepreneur's control: winning the government contract to convert the currency.

We will have to start over and look for a better delivery system. How about this: To deliver the colored money exchange system (let's call it CME), we could begin with the celebrity-endorsement SDM, then branch out into facilities management. In this instance, our first step would be to make a product that could be attached to paper money without defacing it—say, a small tin clip like the ones museums hand out to those who enter. The clip would be stamped with a message or symbol to show that the bill to which it is attached was *not* used to pay for drugs (see Figure 8.1).

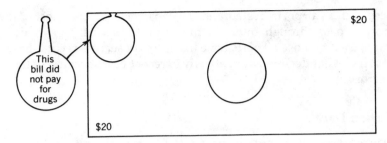

**Figure 8-1.**

The entrepreneurial company would pay for the production of millions of these clips with donations from wealthy concerned individuals and corporations. That is *celebrity endorsement*—having a dozen of the most respected Americans lend their names to the CME project.

The clips would be given to commercial and savings banks in a test community. The banks would give the clips out to customers, retail businesses, community groups, schools, churches, and cultural institutions with the intent of having 100 percent utilization. Celebrity endorsement would assist in gaining broad acceptance of the CME project, and the entrepreneur would generate publicity.

As ancillary support, a CME *newsletter* would provide information as to how well the plan is working. The entrepreneurial company could also run a currency-design contest. Dances and concerts could be sponsored, as well as parades. With the test community running smoothly, the entrepreneurial company could undertake *facilities-management* contracts with other cities to introduce the same kind of credibility-building CME programs there. The cash flow would build significantly, enabling the company to produce prototype currency and to demonstrate to the federal government its ability to produce new currency and get it into the banking system. To make the company an ongoing proposition rather than a one-shot deal, the currency would have to be changed at random every so often until drug dealers gave up their trade.

## TERRORISM

### Problem Formulation

Representatives of religious and political revolutionary groups, principally from various nations in the Middle East, occasionally enter other countries and kill innocent people with bombs or guns, usually in public places such as airports, restaurants, or department stores. Most of these terrorists pass through international airports. Security methods and devices used in those airports have had a spotty success record. International travel has declined dramatically in recent years because of the fear of terrorism.

## Solution Development

Governments have generally responded to terrorist attacks with economic sanctions and, occasionally, military attacks. Neither solution has had a lasting effect on the problem of terrorism. Economic sanctions in particular have been ineffective, because unless all nations join in a sanction, the terrorist country can simply look elsewhere for supplies and markets. Granted, in some instances, nations have joined together in enacting sanctions against a terrorist country, but such groups have an innate weakness: they constitute a cartel, and as Milton Friedman has explained, it is in the nature of cartels to disagree and break up. The Organization of Petroleum Exporting Countries is an excellent example. Thus an economic-sanction cartel cannot stay intact for very long. One member will bolt when the profit for so doing exceeds the cost of upsetting the other members of the cartel. So much for the effectiveness of economic sanctions and military attacks.

## Solution Delivery Method

The *high-technology* SDM could be successful in preventing a great number of terrorist attacks. Since many terrorists are recruited from Palestine Liberation Organization (PLO) training camps in Libya and other Middle Eastern nations, and since any self-contained camp would have a distinctive scent, these terrorists must carry that scent with them when they travel to another country for the purpose of staging an attack. Using present technology, the entrepreneur could develop a microchip-based sensor programmed to pick up the scent of a PLO terrorist training camp. Several hundred of these sensors—costing, say, $20 each—could be placed near the entrance and exit gates of the airports through which terrorists most often travel, and throughout other public places that are vulnerable to attack. When a person carrying the scent of a training camp passes by a sensor, a camera would automatically photograph him or her. At the same time an alarm would alert security guards to the presence of a terrorist. The suspect would immediately be detained and questioned.

Additional revenues could be generated by leasing the cameras and the alarm system to clients and by using the *newsletter-seminar* SDM to train airport personnel and to circulate information about the system to users.

## UNEMPLOYMENT IN OLDER INDUSTRIES

### Problem Formulation

The movement of American industry away from manufacturing steel, oil, and chemical-based products and toward information-related products has created large pockets of unemployment in eastern and midwestern cities. Former steelworkers, for example, are ill-suited for other semi-skilled positions, and the employment opportunities in their communities are relatively few.

### Solution Development

It is unlikely that this army of unemployed men and women can be re-trained successfully as word and data processors for corporate America, but they *can* be retrained as small-business owners, franchisees, and salespersons in direct sales organizations. Commission selling is frequently more lucrative than other forms of employment, and small businesses have been providing satisfactory livelihoods for years.

### Solution Delivery Method

The entrepreneur can assist unemployed men and women to do any one of the following:

1. Buy a local franchise
2. Become a local dealer or representative for a nationally distributed product
3. Buy or establish a local small business and manage its growth and development

The entrepreneurial company—call it Retread, Inc.—develops a system for relating aptitude tests to personal occupational skills. Using the *newsletter-seminar* SDM, Retread invites out-of-work people to come to a conference room downtown where, for a fee of $10, they will take a preliminary aptitude test and discuss the work they would like to do. Those who enjoy the networking experience and find it helpful can pay an up-front fee of $500 for five sessions, during which they will receive all of the following:

- A complete aptitude test
- A test of their adaptability to the fields in which they have the strongest aptitudes
- Training in business and accounting
- Analysis of various available franchises, local businesses for sale, and dealership opportunities
- Assistance in purchasing the franchise, dealer territory, or local business

Retread can also provide equity-linked loans to particularly well-qualified businesspeople, and it can earn additional revenues from one or more of the following sources:

1. Newsletter ads from franchisors and national selling organizations
2. Career-change videotapes, books, and audiocassettes sold through the newsletter or from a booth during the seminars
3. Sale of newsletter articles for use as Sunday supplement features to local newspapers
4. Mailing list rental
5. Facilities management of the potential retread problems of large corporations *before* they abandon a plant

The problem of unemployment in older industries, in other words, can be solved by applying several SDMs—*newsletter-seminar, franchise,* and *facilities management,* to start with. As you continue to think about solving this problem, you might come up with a couple more.

Again, as in so many entrepreneurial endeavors, you are *helping* people when you solve a problem like this. You're not only helping them to earn a livelihood; you're also giving them hope, self-respect, and dignity. And that, really, is what entrepreneuring is all about.

## STEPPARENTING

### Problem Formulation

Children are involved in about half of the remarriages that follow divorce. As the divorce rate has risen, so has the number of stepparents.

These people need solutions to the problems they face in their relationships with the children they have acquired through marriage.

## Solution Development

Family therapy is the usual means of addressing stepparenting problems, but this solution doesn't lend itself to an entrepreneurial delivery. The entrepreneur in this instance should isolate the problems that are shared by large numbers of stepparents and that can be addressed through self-help methods.

Weight Watchers International was able to treat the problem of being overweight by utilizing retail locations and self-help products. EST and other self-actualization companies have been successful in treating more than one person at a time. Perhaps stepparenting problems can be treated in groups as well, using supplementary products and services.

## Solution Delivery Method

The *newsletter-seminar* SDM, with the emphasis on seminars, appears to be the most likely choice for solving stepparenting problems. For a fee, stepparents can attend seminars held in conveniently located conference rooms. At these meetings, they will discuss their problems in groups led by family therapists over an eight- to ten-week period. Together they will arrive at solutions, which they will try out at home. At the next meeting, those solutions can be reevaluated and reissued.

Here the entrepreneur will benefit from additional revenue-generating sources: videotapes, audiocassettes, books, and newsletter subscriptions sold during each seminar.

Two other SDMs come to mind here:

1. A *cookie cutter* roll-out in other cities, where family therapists can be contracted to conduct similar conferences.
2. A *franchise* arrangement in those instances where the demand for seminars is very widespread.

## EXCESSIVE COST AND INEFFECTIVENESS OF THE U.S. PENAL SYSTEM

### Problem Formulation

There are currently 750,000 people behind bars in the United States, up forty percent from 1981. It costs taxpayers $7.2 billion a year to care for them—nearly $100,000 per prisoner per annum, or $280 per prisoner per day. The Pierre Hotel in New York is a bargain compared to one of the government's minimum-luxury residences. With sixty percent of the nation's prisons under court order to remedy inhumane conditions, an unprecedented $3.5-billion-a-year prison construction boom is in progress. Yet, even with the additional facilities that this money will buy, there will not be enough space for prisoners. The resultant overcrowding will in many instances lead to violence and will make it difficult (or impossible) to train prisoners to become productive citizens. The end result will be an extremely high rate of recidivism.

## Solution Development

Several entrepreneurial solutions come to mind, all of them workable:

1. A prison system could be purchased outright by an entrepreneur and converted into a profit-making manufacturing facility.
2. An entrepreneur could contract to run a prison system for the current budget.
3. The entrepreneurial company could produce an electronic device that would make it unnecessary to imprison nonviolent criminals.

Those entrepreneurs who attempt to introduce the first two solutions will run into institutional barriers. That may mitigate the attractiveness of the solutions, but both are doable nonetheless.

## Solution Delivery Modalities

We'll take these three different solutions one at a time and see how they could be put into effect. The first one is the *leveraged buy-out* SDM. It could be used with prisons pretty much the same way it is now being used with hospitals. This would solve the problem of the excessive cost of imprisonment and at the same time would give prisoners a chance to do productive work, learn a trade, and prepare themselves for life outside the walls.

The second SDM, of course, is *facilities management*. In Chapter 7, I mentioned Jack Massey who is successfully managing the penal system for the state of Tennessee under a facilities-management contract.

The third SDM, currently being tested in Wisconsin, is a *high-technology* start-up. It involves a microchip-based transmitter worn by the prisoner, on an ankle bracelet, plus a receiver, which is placed at the door of a nonviolent prisoner's home. The device is connected via telephone lines with a nearby police precinct. Twice a day, when the prisoner leaves for work and again on returning home, the electronic signal is triggered. If the prisoner fails to send out the expected signal, a parole officer visits the home. If this happens a second time, the prisoner returns to jail.

Although this solution has a high-tech basis, its success will depend on a combination of innovation and marketing, not innovation alone. Perhaps retired or moonlighting police officers could be hired and trained to sell the system to prisons and jails.

## HIGH COST OF LEGAL AID

### Problem Formulation

Since 1970 there has been an increase in the number of lawyers and in the aggregate revenues of the legal system. Lawyers are increasingly required to explain the complex laws enacted by our legislators, many of whom are lawyers themselves. In 1970 there were 355,242 lawyers in the United States; in 1983 there were 542,204. The average income of lawyers increased 120 percent over that thirteen-year period.

### Solution Development

An entrepreneurial company could accept some of the risk of litigation and earn a profit if it is successful in reducing the cost of litigation. The model for this company is the health maintenance organization (HMO), which has become an effective means of reducing health care costs in recent years.

### Solution Delivery Method

Two SDMs would have to be combined to build a litigation maintenance organization (LMO): (1) *prepaid subscription* and (2) *tollgate.*

At the outset, individuals and companies would be offered a chance to join the LMO on a prepaid-subscription basis. In return for a fee of, say, $250 a year, the LMO would handle their legal problems without charge for that one year. Using the subscription money, the LMO could then purchase the services of attorneys for a fixed annual fee, the aggregate of which would be seventy-five to eighty percent of the LMO's annual revenues. In the event of major litigation, the LMO would buy a reinsurance policy to lay off the risk.

With steady growth, the LMO could later begin to act as a tollgate on the highway between those who need legal service and those who provide that service. The tollgate company would accept some of the risk to mitigate rising legal costs. It would also train its subscribers to avoid problems, disputes, and litigation. An increased population of lawyers means that many attorneys would flock to LMOs to ensure revenues, and it would be in their best interest to hold down costs in order to have their contract with the LMO renewed—that is, they would be encouraged to negotiate early settlements rather than engage in protracted negotiations leading to a trial.

## DIFFICULTY OF COMMUTING TO WORK

### Problem Formulation

Every weekday, millions of commuters head for work by train, bus, or automobile. New York City alone has some three million daily commuters. Chicago, Los Angeles, Boston, Philadelphia, and other large cities also pose problems for thousands of people who travel to and from their jobs. The cost of a difficult commute is high: pollution, stress, safety hazards, expense, fuel consumption, and unproductive traveling time. The only real attempts at solutions have been in the form of government interference—widening highways, building new access routes, running the railroads—and have served only to encourage more people to drive to work.

### Solution Development

In devising a solution to the commutation problem, we might as well start by eliminating those that would not work. Helicopters, for example, might readily come to mind, but they're too expensive, and it would take too many of them to move the large numbers of people we are talking about here. Buses and trains are already in operation. Some of them are effective; others are not. Private cars cause more problems than they solve. Car pools might work in some instances, but people dislike them, for the most part, and will go to great lengths to avoid them.

What about water transportation? The hovercraft has been put to excellent use in Hong Kong, a city that poses monumental commutation problems. Well implemented, it could work in the United States.

### Solution Delivery Method

The use of hovercrafts to solve commutation problems is a *capital equipment* SDM marketed on a *prepaid subscription* basis. A hovercraft can carry several hundred people at the same cost required to transport ten or so passengers by helicopter. Since most major U.S. cities are built on rivers or harbors, water travel represents a sensible way to move people from the suburbs to the city and back, or from one part of a city to another. In New York, for example, commuters could subscribe to one of several hovercraft routes: up and down the Hudson River, along the East River, through Long Island Sound, or back and forth across the rivers and the harbor. Numerous hovercraft could dock at both ends of, say, 42nd Street, the World Trade Center, and South Street, near the financial district.

The advantages of the hovercraft are considerable. A hovercraft, for example, travels faster than a commuter train and does not require costly tracks and track maintenance. Passengers could buy coffee and doughnuts on board, get a shoeshine, read their newspapers, and arrive at work stress-free in half the time of their present commute. Affluent passengers could buy interests in their community hovercraft, deduct operating costs and depreciation, and lease the hovercraft back to the entrepreneur.

The entrepreneur who sets out to establish a hovercraft service, however, is likely to run into barriers set up by local government or by various labor unions. He or she should plan ahead with this firmly in mind. See PERT chart next page.

## STRESS

### Problem Formulation

It appears that stress is not only an emotional problem but a cause of physiological problems as well. Corporate employees complain of stress caused by the "invisible hand" that makes decisions for them. Families are being asked to carry the emotional load of all the members without the assistance of churches and extended families who previously bore some of the responsibility. The result is stress on all family members.

### Solution Development

Psychotherapists have developed a number of ways to mitigate stress at the corporate and family levels. It may be possible to synthesize their formulas and methods and distribute them by means of videocassettes, audiocassettes, and instruction materials for use by corporations, schools, and families.

## PERT: Hovercraft Service

| Months: | 1 | 2 | 3 | 4 | 5 |
|---|---|---|---|---|---|
| **Finances:** | Meet with family, friends; begin writing business plan | Raise family funds | | | |
| **Service:** | | Assess geographic routes, implications for high-speed waterborne craft | Investigate alternate routes, terminal locations, travel time advantages | Determine optimal route(s), terminal location(s) | Prepare prelim. route feasibility study |
| **Facilities and equipment:** | Use dining room table | Get capital costs on dis-built hovercrafts, hydrofoils, monohulls, multihulls | Get costs on terminal leasing, construction availability | Get operating costs on craft | Meet with craft vendors; plan craft specifications |
| **People:** | Interview engineering, legal, marketing consultants, traffic engineer | Hire engineering, legal, mktg. consultants; additional interviews | Hire traffic engineer | | |
| **Administration:** | Incorporate; devise logo, stationery | Review statutes, regs; consult council of governments, OAG, Amtrak, bus lines, etc. | Consult Chamber of Commerce; Department of Ferry, State Department of Transportation, census tracts | | |
| **Marketing:** | Assess route demographics political, environ. considerations | Investigate competitive modes: express buses, commuter rail, etc.; estimate ridership, travel time; plan market survey | Determine total potential travel demand; conduct market surveys | Conduct additional market surveys | Complete market surveys; determine market capture, fare structure |

| Months: | 6 | 7 | 8 | 9 | 10 |
|---|---|---|---|---|---|
| Finances: | Vendor signs interim agreement to provide credit | Complete, submit business plan to federal ship financing authorities; obtain balloon permit | Meet with maritime officials, banks, SBA, BDC, IDA | Proceed with due diligence | Additional due diligence |
| Service: | Construct mathematical transportation model | | | | |
| Facilities and equipment: | Complete cost specifications for craft construction | | | | Sign berthing facilities lease |
| People: | | | | | |
| Administration: | Submit plan to Coast Guard, Department of Ferry; prepare construction PERT chart | Engage in open dialogue with Coast Guard, Department of Ferry | Coast Guard, Department of Ferry approves plan | | |
| Marketing: | Evaluate other sources of revenue: food, beverages, advertising, freight, charters | Complete evaluation of other sources of revenue | Meet with assemblymen, borough presidents re: berthing lease | Lobby support of government officials; seek endorsements | Meet with mayor, city controller |

137

*PERT: Hovercraft Service (Continued)*

| Months: | 11 | 12–16 | 17 | 18 | 19 |
|---|---|---|---|---|---|
| Finances: | Close deal; maritime administration guarantees 87 1/2 percent of bank loan | | Modify, submit business plan to investment banks | Meet with investment bankers; proceed with due diligence | Additional due diligence |
| Service: | | | Plan sporadic sample runs; request proposals from caterers, in-flight publishers | Complete construction; caterers, publishers submit proposals | Begin sample runs; evaluate proposals |
| Facilities and equipment: | Begin construction of two identical craft | Additional construction | Reserve berthing facilities for sample runs | | |
| People: | | | Interview captain, chief engr., request proposals from advert. consultants | Additional interviews; advertising consultants submit ad campaign proposals | Hire captain, chief engineer; evaluate ad campaign proposals |
| Administration: | Establish inspection schedule for builder and Coast Guard | | | | |
| Marketing: | | | | | |

| Months: | 20 | 21 | 22 | 23 | 24 | 25 |
|---|---|---|---|---|---|---|
| Finances: | Additional due diligence | Structure sale-leaseback tax shelter | Investment bank retails tax shelter units through suburban stockbrokers | Stockbrokers sell tax shelter units | Stockbrokers sell additional tax shelter units | Raise finances from sale-leaseback |
| Service: | Complete specified sample runs; select caterer, publisher | | Commence commuter operations | Debug operations | Plan weekend charter trips | Order additional crafts |
| Facilities and equipment: | Get costs from crane operators for haulouts necessitated by floating garbage underneath | Contract with crane operators | Use existing facilities or floating barges, catwalks | | | |
| People: | Hire advertising agency | Interview bos'n, assistant engineer, cabin attendants | Seek board of directors | | | |
| Administration: | | Coast Guard certifies craft | Distribute questionnaires on board | | | |
| Marketing: | Advertising agency revises ad campaign; revise fare structure | Commence ad campaign, sell prepaid subscriptions; prepare questionnaires | Continue ad campaign as regular expense | | Determine fleet, route expansion schedule | |

## Solution Delivery Method

This problem suggests two SDMs: (1) a *newsletter-seminar* method for corporations and (2) a *cookie-cutter* SDM for families. The newsletter-seminar method, in this instance, might very well lead to *facilities-management* contracts, making a third SDM feasible.

The newsletter-seminar method would be implemented by a human relations officer, who would counsel corporate personnel who are under unusual stress or who are responding badly to ordinary corporate stress. The pyramid launch discussed in Chapter 7 will serve as a good model for this project.

The entrepreneur who wishes to work with families could launch a cookie-cutter stress-counseling business. A good first step here might be to hire therapists in various cities to conduct stress-mitigation conferences during the evenings and perhaps on occasional weekends.

Both methods would be financed up front by clients. As a result, the entrepreneur would not require much venture capital, nor would he or she have to give away revenues as does a franchisor. Nevertheless, *franchising* should not be dismissed as a means of delivering stress-reducing therapy. That method constitutes a fourth possible SDM for this problem. See PERT chart next page.

## WASTE MANAGEMENT

### Problem Formulation

As the population of the United States increases, so does the amount of waste produced every day. Some of these mountains of trash are hauled away to landfills, others are burned, and large amounts are buried or dumped into the ocean. But waste is not all that easy to get rid of. It washes back to shore, polluting our beaches, or it seeps back up to the surface of the earth or into the groundwater, endangering people's lives. This problem grows larger each day as our society generates more and more waste in need of disposal.

### Solution Development

The solution appears to be entrepreneurial—that is, if there is a sufficiently attractive incentive to remove waste efficiently, that task will be accomplished. The law of reciprocity argues for that.

People wish to be rid of waste without thinking about it. Thus the solution mechanism should involve them very little. The entrepreneur should remove the waste effectively and be paid an amount equal to the present cost of the waste problem.

*PERT: Stress Reduction Therapy Centers*

| Months: | 1 | 2 | 3 | 4 | 5 |
|---|---|---|---|---|---|
| Finances: | Meet with family, friends; Begin writing business plan | | | Complete, submit business plan to local banks, SBA; Finance printing costs, mailing | Meet with bankers, SBA, etc. Deposit 400 checks |
| Service: | | | Solicit articles, book reviews, pieces for newsletter | Solicit additional pieces | Design layout, running title, oversized appearance |
| Facilities and equipment: | Use dining room table, typewriter | | | | Look for seminar location, caterers |
| People: | Locate prominent stress therapists, MDs, nutritionists | Negotiate with experts; interview printer | Retain experts for editorial board, articles, products, services; hire printer | | Hire secretary, bookkeeper |
| Administration: | Incorporate; devise logo, stationery | | Add editorial board to letterhead | Mail 2,000 pieces | Establish bookkeeping procedures; pay printer |
| Marketing: | Write mission sheet, "welcome to our company" | Get 2,000 names of personnel directors; consult primary sources, D&B | Write, design direct-mail piece; consult additional mailing list sources | Complete mailing list; solicit advertising (e.g., luggage companies, airlines) | Subscriber list of 400 |

*PERT: Stress Reduction Therapy Centers (Continued)*

| Months: | 6 | 7 | 8 | 9 | 10 |
|---|---|---|---|---|---|
| Finances: | Subscribers finance newsletter | | | | |
| Service: | First issue ready | Solicit seminar products; consider speakers | Invite seminar speakers | Solicit appearances from authors of "Speak Out" | Audiocassette ready: "the mobile manager's family in tow" |
| Facilities and equipment: | Compare costs; book location, caterers | Look for office, next seminar location | Get costs for audio-video services; book hotel, catering | Hire audio-video services; rent office; look for next seminar location | Use professional recording studio; book hotel, caterers |
| People: | Interview managing editor | Hire managing editor | | Interview chief administrative officer | Additional interviews; interview trainers |
| Administration: | Mail first monthly issues; pay deposit for seminar hall | | Mail 2,000 additional direct mail pieces; amend incorporation statement as producer, distributor, analyst | Order seminar products from publishers | |
| Marketing: | Promote "speak out" column for reader participation | Get 2,000 additional names; scour publishing industry for seminar products and ideas | Negotiate contract for wholesale books, etc. | Announce month 12 seminar: "Understanding Relocation Stress" | Advertise seminar in newsletter, related newsletters; prepare questionnaire |

| Months: | 11 | 12 | 13 | 14 |
|---|---|---|---|---|
| Finances: | | | | |
| Service: | Videocassette ready: 'prepping the mobile manager' | Hold 2-day seminar; videotape workshops | Administer 10 1-day analyses; solicit articles for second newsletter on general stress | Administer 10 additional consulting contracts; hold second 2-day seminar |
| Facilities and equipment: | Use professional studio | Use comfortable hotel; decide on second office location | Look for second office | Use comfortable hotel; rent second office |
| People: | Hire chief administrative officer; additional interviews | Hire trainers | Interview office-sales manager | Hire office-sales manager, secretary |
| Administration: | Establish financial control system, next 12 months' budget | Distribute questionnaires at seminar; mail 2,000 additional direct-mail pieces | Index problems and proposed solutions | |
| Marketing: | Announce month 14 seminar; additional advertisements for month 12 seminar; get 2,000 additional names | Offer $1,000 1-day analysis, $25,000 performance contracts; sell products at back of room | Advertise seminar cassettes and products to nonattendees; announce month 16 seminar | Sell seminar videos, newsletter articles to cable, network TV, newspapers, etc. |

PERT: *Stress Reduction Therapy Centers* (Continued)

| Months: | 15 | 16 | 17 | 18 | 19–20 |
|---|---|---|---|---|---|
| Finances: | | | | | |
| Service: | Begin work on 2 performance contracts; design layout of "stress" | Hold third 2-day seminar; first issue of "stress" ready | | | |
| Facilities and equipment: | Look for seminar locations, caterers | | | | |
| People: | Hire additional secretary | | | | |
| Administration: | Insert renewal letters in 10th issue | Mail first "mini" issue of "stress" as a bonus to renewing clientele | Mail 20,000 pieces | | |
| Marketing: | Prepare subscription renewal letters, advertise seminar cassettes to nonattendees | Get 20,000 names; design direct-mail piece | Complete mailing list direct-mail piece | | Target neighborhood therapists |

## Solution Delivery Method

The SDM that would work best here, I think, is *facilities management*. The entrepreneur could sign waste-removal contracts with cities, apartment buildings, restaurants, plants, or residential neighborhoods. The agreements could be like the other facilities-management arrangements we have discussed: the entrepreneur would agree to remove all waste for the exact amount now budgeted for that purpose. If he or she can get the job done faster and more efficiently than the previous carter, the resulting profits would constitute the reward.

Some of the waste could be reprocessed as energy or recycled paper, some could be incinerated, and some used as landfill. All of it must be disposed of in the safest, least polluting way possible. See PERT chart next page.

# MISUSE OF ALCOHOL AND DRUGS BY TEENAGERS

## Problem Formulation

It is estimated that one in five adolescents in the United States regularly drink alcohol, smoke marijuana, use cocaine, or ingest or inject other harmful drugs. The problem is not an urban or suburban one; it is national in scope. A pusher may acquire his inventory in a metropolitan area and sell it in high school parking lots as easily in small towns as in large ones.

## Solution Development

The problem is one of arrested moral development among adolescents. Several decades ago parents would stress the difference between good and evil and be supported in their instruction by the church, school, and community service groups and clubs. In the present more complex society, however, the family is often a weaker institution, due to divorce, frequent relocation, or other factors. The other support mechanisms are either unavailable or not used by the family. As a result there is an entrepreneurial opportunity to teach teenagers about the dangers of alcohol and drug abuse.

## Solution Delivery Method

Teenagers are not likely to go out on their own in search of information about drug abuse. The knowledge can be made available to them, however, if it's packaged attractively and presented at school, during

*PERT: Waste Management*

| Months: | 1 | 2 | 3 | 4 | 5 | 6 |
|---|---|---|---|---|---|---|
| Finances: | Meet with family, friends; begin writing business plan | Raise family, friends' funds | Complete, submit business plan to local banks, SBA, BDC, IDA, etc.; staff defers wages | Meet with local banks, SBA, BDC, IDA, etc. | Take out small loan | |
| Product: | | | Begin operations, R&D—research intensive | Additional R&D | Develop operations strategy | Additional R&D; complete operations strategy |
| Facilities and equipment: | Use dining room table | | | | | |
| People: | Interview civil, industrial engineers, cost accountant, legal consultant | Interview engineers; hire legal consultant | Hire engineers, cost accountant | | Hire secretary | |
| Administration: | | Review legal issues, liabilities | | | | Get costs for key man, liability insurance |
| Marketing: | | Target communities planning or constructing waste management facilities | Target additional communities | Write mission sheet, "welcome to our company" | Revise promotional literature; look for requests for proposals (RFPs) | Look for additional RFPs; prepare detailed proposal/bid |

| Months: | 7 | 8 | 9 | 10 | 11 | 12 |
|---|---|---|---|---|---|---|
| Finances: | | | | | | |
| Product: | | | | | | |
| Facilities and equipment: | | | | | | Look for office |
| People: | | | | | | Offer employment to existing plant operators |
| Administration: | | | | | | |
| Marketing: | Complete, submit detailed proposal/bid | Lobby local leaders, community groups, news media | Interview with blue-ribbon committee | Interview with town council; perform cost–benefit analysis | Complete cost–benefit analysis with town council, mayor | Mayor signs 5-year operations contract with renewal option |

## PERT: Waste Management (Continued)

| Months: | 13 | 14 | 15 | 16 | 17 | 18 |
|---|---|---|---|---|---|---|
| Finances: | | | | | | |
| Product: | | | | | | |
| Facilities and equipment: | Purchase automatic dialing alarm system for plant; rent office | Install security system | Commence new plant operations; manage inspection, cleanup, dismantlement, auction of old plant | Operate plant; build track record; satisfied customers | | |
| People: | Hire bookkeeper | Interview additional plant operators (new plant is larger) | Hire plant operators | | Interview civil engineering R&D team | Additional interviews |
| Administration: | Establish daily bookkeeping routine | | "Passing of the baton"—assume operational control | | | |
| Marketing: | | | | | | |

| Months: | 19 | 20–23 | 24 | 25 | 26 | 27 |
|---|---|---|---|---|---|---|
| Finances: | New staff defers wages | | | Complete, submit business plan to banks, credit companies | Meet with banks, credit companies; proceed with due diligence | Additional due diligence |
| Product: | Begin R&D—develop waste-to-energy plant design | Additional R&D | Additional R&D | Complete 100-ton waste-to-energy plant design | | |
| Facilities and equipment: | | | | | | |
| People: | Hire engineering R&D team | | | | | |
| Administration: | | Review community performance, zoning ordinances | Review community performance, zoning ordinances | | Submit plans to Department of Environmental Protection, Air Bureau | Engage in open dialogue with regulatory agencies |
| Marketing: | | Target communities undergoing solid waste crises | Target additional communities; look for RFPs | Look for additional RFPs; prepare detailed proposal/bid; revise promo. literature | Complete, submit detailed proposal/bid; prepare slide show | Lobby local leaders, community groups, news media; pursue energy market |

149

*PERT: Waste Management (Continued)*

| Months: | 28 | 29 | 30 | 31 | 32 | 33 |
|---|---|---|---|---|---|---|
| Finances: | Structure financing to cover construction, interest during construction, legal, financial fees | Sign interim agreement with credit company | | Apply for UDAG | | Raise capital |
| Product: | | | | | | |
| Facilities and equipment: | | | | | | |
| People: | | | | | | |
| Administration: | | | | Regulatory agencies submit final comments, approvals; apply to HUD | | Receive permits |
| Marketing: | Interview with blue-ribbon committee; show slides of dangerous landfills, antiquated equipment | Interview with town council; perform cost–benefit analysis | Complete cost–benefit analysis with town council, mayor | Sign interim agreement with town council, steam-run factories, utilities | Town council holds public hearings | Mayor signs plant construction/management contract |

community events, at camp, after club meetings, and in other places where teenagers gather.

The SDM to use here, I'd say, is the *celebrity-endorsed consumer product* launch. You would start by persuading several well-known and highly regarded actors, athletes, and musicians to appear in a series of video-tapes designed to educate teenagers about the real and immediate dangers of substance abuse as well as the long-term consequences such as brain damage and social alienation (the rap group, Run DMC, is currently participating in a similar plan). Celebrities with easily recognizable voices might contribute to audiocassette presentations of similar material. Even conventional classroom materials such as pamphlets and other printed material would be more attractive to teenagers if celebrity photographs and quotations were liberally sprinkled throughout. You could market these materials to corporations and institutions, which would pay for their production and distribution and receive credit thereby.

These educational tapes and booklets might include material on "temptation management." They could also be designed to make the teenagers aware of the ways in which some motion pictures and TV programs treat drug use and drinking as accepted social customs, or suggest a "need" for a drink whenever things go slightly wrong. Your materials might go on to encourage teenagers to take action against such TV shows or movies by stating their objections in letters to the station or the distributor.

The entrepreneur can grow the company by producing and distributing similar products for prisoners, juvenile delinquents, and vandals. The follow-on entrepreneurial opportunities include *newsletter-seminar, prepaid subscription,* and *facilities management.*

Earlier in this chapter we discussed the possible use of celebrity endorsement to launch an entrepreneurial solution to teenage crime. This antidrug entrepreneurship might lead to, result from, or be combined with that anticrime effort. See PERT chart next page.

## HIGH COST OF COLLEGE TUITION

### Problem Formulation

The cost of a college education quadrupled in the 1970s, rising from $10,000 in 1970 to $40,000 in 1983. In the mid-1980s, costs continue to rise, and colleges work furiously to solicit alumni contributions to supplement tuition, which cannot cover all expenses.

PERT: *Celebrity-Endorsed Substance Abuse Program*

| Months: | 1 | 2 | 3 | 4 | 5 |
|---|---|---|---|---|---|
| Finances: | Meet with family, friends; begin writing business plan | Raise family funds | Complete, submit business plan to local banks, SBA, BDC, IDA | Meet with bankers, SBA, BDC, IDA | Celebrities accept royalties on future sales |
| Product: | | | Design temptation management kits, audio/videotapes; solicit ideas from board of education | Solicit articles from board of education for sample newsletter for "Club" | Complete design of temptation management kit, audio/video scripts |
| Facilities and equipment: | Use dining room table | | | | Get costs on professional audio/video services |
| People: | Locate child psychologist, experts in drug counseling, psychology, etc. | Interview child psychologist, experts | Hire child psychologist, retain experts for editorial boards; assemble celebrity "hit list" | Meet with celebs (e.g., Prince, Dave Winfield) and their agents | Negotiate with celebs |
| Administration: | Incorporate; devise logo, stationery | | Add editorial board, employees to balance of letterhead | Print and mail promo literature to celebs and their agents | |
| Marketing: | | Write mission sheet, "welcome to our company" | Revise promo literature | Complete promo literature | Target corp. sponsors (e.g., Kimberly-Clark) |

| Months: | 6 | 7 | 8 | 9 | 10 | 11 |
|---|---|---|---|---|---|---|
| Finances: | | | Sponsors finance audio/video cassettes | Sponsors finance marketing and distribution of products/services | | |
| Product: | Prepare sample temptation management kit, newsletter | Solicit longer articles, book reviews, case histories for newsletter | | Produce "temptation management" products | First newsletter ready—use as promotional device | Audio cassette ready: "I'm hip, I'm high, I just touched the sky" |
| Facilities and equipment: | | | | Hire professional audio/video services; look for office | Rent office | |
| People: | Contract with celebs to be role models; hire secretary | Interview marketing vice president | Additional interviews | Hire marketing vice president, printer; seek board of directors from sponsors | Hire bookkeeper | |
| Administration: | | | | | Establish bookkeeping procedures | |
| Marketing: | Contact sponsors, give presentations | Negotiate with sponsors | Additional negotiations | Contact with bellwether sponsors; media announcement | Target PTAs, rehab centers, religious organizations, summer camps, private schools, etc. | Contact school boards, PTAs, etc.; appear on "Good Morning America" |

*PERT: Celebrity-Endorsed Substance Abuse Program (Continued)*

| Months: | 12 | 13 | 14 | 15 | 16 | 17 |
|---|---|---|---|---|---|---|
| Finances: | | | | | | |
| Product: | Videocassette ready: "Downright upright tonight—hungover tomorrow" | Hold first meetings with adolescents | Solicit seminar products; consider speakers; hold additional meetings | Invite seminar speakers; hold additional meetings | Hold additional meetings | Audio cassettes ready: "here's looking at you, sober" |
| Facilities and equipment: | | Look for seminar location, caterers; decide on office location | Compare costs; book motel, caterers; look for second office | Look for next seminar location; rent second office | Compare costs; book location, caterers | Look for third seminar location; decide on third office location |
| People: | Form board of directors; interview managing editor | Hire managing editor, interview office/sales mgr. | Interview national networking manager; additional interviews | Hire office/sales manager, secretary; recruit school nurse, directors for "battle" | Hire national networking manager | |
| Administration: | | Initial board meeting | | | | |
| Marketing: | Contact sweepstakes suppliers, advertisers; (e.g., Disneyland/ ROTC) | Contract with school district board, sweepstakes suppliers, advertisers | Announce, advertise "go for it" camping/hiking weekends, all-night hike marathons | Announce, advertise "no alcohol/ drugs battle of the bands," "mobile disco" | Announce 8-week seminar course | Advertise in newsletter, related newsletters; write questionnaire |

| Months: | 18 | 19 | 20 | 21 | 22 | 23 |
|---|---|---|---|---|---|---|
| **Finances:** | | | | | | |
| **Product:** | Video cassettes ready; "natural highs" | Begin 3-hour seminars, videotape seminars | Hold "battle of the bands" | Hold weekend camping/hiking "in association with the Sierra Club"; additional seminars | Hold "mobile disco" nights | |
| **Facilities and equipment:** | Compare costs, book motel, caterers; look for third office | Use conveniently located motel; serve doughnuts, coffee; rent third office | Local schools provide "battle of the bands" facilities; bands bring their own equipment | Use conveniently located motel for seminar; serve doughnuts/ coffee | Local schools provide gyms; rent equipment | |
| **People:** | | Neighborhood therapists participate; hire office/ sales manager | Recruit adolescents to sell buttons, posters, T-shirts | Neighborhood therapists participate; hire adolescent to organize "mobile day" | Interview list broker | Hire list broker |
| **Administration:** | | | | | | |
| **Marketing:** | Advertise in local newspapers; revise questionnaires | Sell subscriptions, products at back of seminar room | Sell buttons, posters, T-shirts at "battle of the bands" | | | Market list to *Boys Life*, *Seventeen*, direct mail advertisers, etc. |

## Solution Development

Great universities with large physical plants and endowments are similar to oil companies and rust-belt industries: their assets are undervalued. Old, once-proud industrial companies, managed by well-meaning but uninvolved boards of directors, have been acquired by leveraged buy-out experts who borrowed on the reappraised values of the companies' assets. A similar situation exists with colleges, but there is another factor in the college-LBO scenario: alumni loyalty.

## Solution Delivery Method

In this instance, the solution could be delivered by means of the *leveraged buy-out,* using a public stock offering to tender for control of a major university. The alumnus, outraged at first that Old Ivy is about to fall into the hands of a "raider," soon realizes that he and his fellow alumni must buy the stock before nonalumni snap it all up. This creates upward pressure on the shares; the raider discloses his plan to manage Old Ivy on a profit-making basis; and a few major alumni donors fall in behind him. They tell the trustees that they can no longer be counted on for major gifts, and the trustees capitulate: Old Ivy begins trading over the counter.

The newly raised cash and the endowment permit Old Ivy's new management to offer attractive cash and stock incentives to attract the best faculty, which in turn attracts the top students. Old Ivy's high-quality research is packaged and sold on a *prepaid subscription* basis, and *newsletters* and *seminars* are offered in areas that are of interest to large numbers of people. Old Ivy eventually generates many new revenue sources from its sale of information in different markets. As cash flow improves, tuitions are reduced per student, but income rises overall as more students are admitted. This SDM has worked before: the success of hospital management companies suggests that college management companies can thrive as well.

## MALE SEXUAL IMPOTENCE

### Problem Formulation

The inability of men to maintain an erection sufficient for satisfactory sexual intercourse is a growing problem. The causes of impotence are both psychological and physiological; they include stress, beta-blockers, chemotherapy, clogged phemeral arteries, and diseases such as diabetes. It is estimated that the problem affects over five million men in America.

## Solution Development

One available solution is an implantable pump that costs approximately $7,500 to insert. This device, however, cannot be removed. It would therefore be a suitable solution only for those men whose impotence is caused by an irreversible physical condition. For other men, who might be impotent only temporarily because of physical or psychological stress, this solution is not viable. Clearly another is needed, and so those entrepreneurs who are interested in solving this problem will have to develop a less expensive, removable solution.

## Solution Delivery Method

Your entrepreneurial company could develop a *high-technology* solution to the problem. Here's one suggestion: a small, heat-sensitive coil, like a small Slinky, could be sewn into the penis beneath the epidermis. The heat of the vagina would cause this device to expand, producing a sufficient erection for intercourse. The product could be removed should normal potency return. Marketing would be directly to urologists, who would be instructed in surgical techniques.

# ROACHES

## Problem Formulation

Cockroaches are ubiquitous; they appear filthy, multiply rapidly, and are very hard to get rid of. They have developed a survival instinct that is second to none.

## Solution Development

Roaches quickly become impervious to poisons in the form of powder and spray. They learn to walk around traps and poisoned areas. As a result, the entrepreneur who wishes to tackle this problem will have to find a more sophisticated solution.

## Solution Delivery Method

A *high-technology* solution again suggests itself—in this instance, a scientific means of blocking the reproductive ability of roaches. In other words, if they cannot be killed, we must prevent them from being born. The reproductive signals and senses of roaches could be altered genetically to cause them to be unable to reproduce. The generating material

*PERT: Roach Control*

| Months: | 1 | 2 | 3 | 4 | 5 |
|---|---|---|---|---|---|
| Finances: | Meet with family, friends; begin writing business plan | Raise family, friends' funds | Apply to foundations, National Science Foundation, etc.; staff defers wages | Complete, submit business plan to local banks, SBA, BDC, IDA, etc. | Modify, submit business plan to investment banker |
| Product: | | | Begin R&D, research intensive | Additional R&D | Additional R&D—achieve consensus on concept |
| Facilities and equipment: | Use dining room table; scientists spread out in university labs | | Continue research in separate labs | Determine central lab location | Use Professor Y's lab as temporary central lab |
| People: | Locate molecular geneticists, entomologists | Interview scientists | Hire core scientific team | Expand scientific team | Retain international "Scientific Sentinels"—contribute casual findings |
| Administration: | Incorporate; devise logo, stationery | | Obtain grant applications; apply for technology transfers, 2nd scientific brainstorm session | Secure technology transfers | Secure additional technology transfers; 2nd brainstorm session |
| Marketing: | | | | | Write mission sheet, "welcome to our company" |

| Months: | 6 | 7 | 8 | 9 | 10 |
|---|---|---|---|---|---|
| Finances: | Introductions made with VCs; proceed with due diligence | Additional due diligence | Complete due diligence structure, R&D, tax shelter | Begin VC road show | Continue VC road show |
| Product: | Additional R&D | | | | |
| Facilities and equipment: | | | | | |
| People: | Hire secretary | Interview chief administrative officer | Additional interviews | Hire chief administrative officer | |
| Administration: | | | | | Establish financial control system |
| Marketing: | | | | | |

*PERT: Roach Control* (*Continued*)

| Months: | 11 | 12 | 13 | 14 | 15 | 16 |
|---|---|---|---|---|---|---|
| Finances: | Continues road show; qualifies lead investor | | | | Close deal; raise capital | |
| Product:<br>Facilities and equipment: | | | | Additional R&D<br>Decide on lab location | Additional R&D<br>Look for lab | Additional R&D<br>Rent lab, equipment and adjoining office |
| People: | Interview lab engineer | Additional interviews | | Hire lab engineer | | Hire lab technicians, secretary, bookkeeper; seek board of directors |
| Administration: | | Establish employee stock option plan | | | | Establish bookkeeping procedures |
| Marketing: | | | Revise promo literature, give "dog and pony shows" to investors | Additional "dog and pony shows" | Final meetings with investors | |

| Months: | 17 | 18 | 19 | 20 | 21 | 22 |
|---|---|---|---|---|---|---|
| Finances: | | | | | | |
| Product: | Additional R&D | Complete prototype, begin alpha tests | Additional alpha tests, debugging; prepare manufacturing feasibility study | Decide on manufacturing | | |
| Facilities and equipment: | Modify equipment | Get costs from university contractor | Hire university lab for feeding studies | | | |
| People: | Interview legal, manufacturing consultants | Form board of directors | | | | |
| Administration: | Present first monthly financial report to stockholders | File patent disclosure | File patent; apply to EPA | Engage in open dialogue with EPA; initial board meeting | | |
| Marketing: | | Perform efficacy studies | Additional efficacy studies | Complete efficacy studies; perform feeding studies | Perform toxicity, mutagenicity, teratogenicity studies | Perform environmental fate, dissipation, accumulation studies |

*PERT: Roach Control* (*Continued*)

| Months: | 23 | 24–35 | 36 | 37 | 38 | 39 |
|---|---|---|---|---|---|---|
| Finances: | | | | Modify, submit business plan to investment bankers for IPO | Meet with investment bankers, proceed with due diligence | Obtain letter of intent for IPO |
| Product: | | | | | | |
| Facilities and equipment: | | | | | Decide on plant location | Look for plant |
| People: | | | | Interview marketing vice president | Additional interviews | Hire marketing vice president |
| Administration: | | | Evaluation of studies | File EPA registration | | EPA approval |
| Marketing: | Perform spray, drift, reentry protection studies | Additional studies | | Complete, analyze, document studies | | Formulate marketing strategy |

could then be sold as a consumer product through supermarkets and drugstores. Purchasers would spray or dust the product in the areas where roaches live.

## POTHOLES

### Problem Formulation

Concrete and asphalt streets and highways break up and potholes form. Cars and trucks roll over the potholes, damaging alignment, chassis, and shock absorbers. Drivers frequently swerve around potholes and scrape their cars or cause accidents.

### Solution Development

Many cities pour hot asphalt into potholes, flatten the asphalt, then let traffic wear it down. However, the traffic recreates the potholes within several weeks. The problem requires more than a Band-Aid℗.

### Solution Delivery Method

One likely entrepreneurial solution is the use of a microwave oven to bake the asphalt into the hole sufficiently to prevent it from collapsing under the weight of traffic. The chemicals in the asphalt may require some modification, but when baked immediately for a few minutes with a microwave oven hung from the back of a truck, the pothole should remain sealed.

The entrepreneurial company should follow the *facilities-management* SDM, agreeing to solve a city's pothole problem for the current budget. If the solution costs less to deliver than the budget allows, the difference will be the entrepreneurial company's profit.

## CARE OF THE AGED

### Problem Formulation

The population of the United States is rapidly growing older. Some fifty years ago, before World War II, forty percent of the U.S. population was under eighteen years old. Now, however, the pendulum has swung the other way, and forty percent of our population is now over age sixty-five. This population shift should suggest several opportunities to you if you are interested in using entrepreneurial methods to help older people.

## PERT: Caring for the Aged

| Months: | 1 | 2 | 3 | 4 | 5 |
|---|---|---|---|---|---|
| Finances: | Meet with family, friends; begin writing business plan | Raise funds | Staff defers wages | | Complete, submit business plan to HUD, mortgage bankers, banks, insurance companies |
| Product: | Plan initial architectural scheme, amenities; request proposals from architects | Architects submit preliminary sketches with amenities: no-skid floors, extra-wide doorways, etc. | Decide on parcel locations, architectural design; get costs on ankle bracelets, motorized golf carts, etc. | Look for parcels; negotiate with ankle bracelet companies, etc. | Decide on parcels; prepare land, site planning: unit density, etc.; sign interim agreement with subcontractors |
| Facilities and equipment: | Use dining room table | | Request proposals from construction companies | Construction companies submit bids | Analyze cost estimates of bids |
| People: | Interview architects, architectural engineer, developer; marketing, legal consultant | Hire marketing, legal consultant; additional interviews | Hire core development team | Hire legal consultant; interview traffic, civil, soil engineering consultants | Hire land planning consulting team |
| Administration: | | Review legal issues; consult with FHA, VA | Review zoning, building ordinances; state contractor's office | | Appraisal, legal survey, title search; prepare deposit receipt, option agreement |
| Marketing: | Conduct primary housing market analysis: define targeted geographical market: consult National Assoc. of Home Builders, etc. | Evaluate proximity to markets, projected housing demand, market capture, competition; conduct market survey | Additional market surveys | Complete market surveys; plan pricing strategy | Analyze soil quality, traffic circulation, utility availability |

| Months: | 6 | 7 | 8 | 9 | 10 |
|---|---|---|---|---|---|
| Finances: | Meet with S&Ls, commercial banks, insurance companies; proceed with due diligence | Additional due diligence | Additional due diligence | Structure acquisition, development, construction loan to cover fees, interest during construction | |
| Product: | Prepare final sketches | | Prepare contract documents: detailed drawings and materials specs | | |
| Facilities and equipment: | Sign interim agreement with general contractor | Property manager suggests locks, hardware, mechanical systems, cash flow projections | Contractor prepares additional cost estimates, construction PERT charts | | |
| People: | Interview property manager-consultant | Hire property manager/consultant | | | |
| Administration: | | Submit initial land development plan to building department, community board | | Engage in open dialogue with building department, community board | Meet with building department, community board |
| Marketing: | Additional feasibility studies | Complete, analyze, document feasibility studies | Redefine target market; reanalyze competition, pricing strategy | Property manager assists in planning, execution of marketing activities | |

PERT: *Caring for the Aged* (Continued)

| Months: | 11 | 12 | 13 | 14 | 15 |
|---|---|---|---|---|---|
| Finances: | Close deal, raise capital | Meet with local hospitals re: services | Negotiate with hospitals for "traveling geriatric" services | Contract with hospitals | |
| Product: | | Begin construction | Additional construction | Additional construction | Additional construction |
| Facilities and equipment: | Look for office | Get costs for trailer, furnishings; rent office | Establish sales compound in on-site trailer; prepare resident guidebooks | Complete resident guidebooks | |
| People: | | Interview special programs coordinator | Additional interviews: interview salespeople | Hire special programs coordinator, salespeople | |
| Administration: | Obtain public approval, performance bond; sign closing; transfer title | Establish meeting schedules with contractor, property manager during "shakedown" period | Establish sales force objectives, compensation, territories; register trademarks | | |
| Marketing: | Prepare promotional literature, brochures | Revise promotional literature | Develop sales kit | | |

| Months: | 16 | 17-25 | 26 | 27 | 28 | 29 |
|---|---|---|---|---|---|---|
| Finances: | | | | | | |
| Product: | First construction phase complete | Additional construction | Additional construction | Complete all construction phases; begin final inspection | Complete inspection | Seniors move in; form senior community council, senior senate, senior-produced newsletter<br>Prepare questionnaires |
| Facilities and equipment: | Decorate sales model | | | | | |
| People: | | | Interview activities director | Additional interviews | Hire activities director, young staff with CPR training<br>Schedule activities: exercise, art classes; library with large print books | |
| Administration: | | | | | | |
| Marketing: | | | | | | |

*PERT: Caring for the Aged* (*Continued*)

| Months: | 30 | 31 | 32 | 33 | 34 | 35 |
|---|---|---|---|---|---|---|
| Finances: | | | | | | |
| Product: | Beta tests | Additional beta tests | Additional beta tests: study property management feedback | Remodel development design | Complete franchise prototype design | Plan franchising agreement: advertising budget, services, complete package |
| Facilities and equipment: | | | | | | |
| People: | | Form focus groups | | Interview cost accountant | Additional interviews | Hire cost accountant |
| Administration: | Distribute questionnaires | | | Establish employee stock option plan | | |
| Marketing: | | | | | | |

## Solution Development

Nursing homes and in-home services are expensive, and most of them are targeted at the very old and those who are unable to care for themselves. However, there is a growing number of people who *are* able to care for themselves but are afraid to live alone. It is these people whom you will be helping by offering an entrepreneurial solution to their problem.

## Solution Delivery Method

To solve the problem of these older people your entrepreneurial company could create for them an environment that is safe, pleasant, and affordable; one in which they will have privacy but not the kind of isolation that would make them afraid.

The SDM you would use here is *prepaid subscription.* The older person, or his or her children, would buy a bond from you, repayable at any time, plus interest, that the older person leaves the residential community. In addition, the older person would provide a like amount of capital to purchase an equity interest in his or her residence, salable when the older person leaves the residential community. You would use the loan as your equity contribution to attract a long-term lender to finance construction of the community. The equity in the residence is used for working capital.

In return, the older people live in a fully electronic community with closed-circuit television to make certain they take any appropriate required medication, golf carts to get to the supermarket, sports facilities, and many other country club-style features. Electronic ankle bracelets would signal to a central switchboard if they were in trouble. The bond and equity would be returned to an older person's estate when he or she leaves the residence. Presumably the community's property values would increase for resale at a higher price in the future, thus providing a capital gain on the equity. A PERT chart begins on page 164.

## GRAFFITI

### Problem Formulation

Vandals continue to deface buildings, monuments, public structures, and vehicles with spray paint, causing an eyesore and diminishing the quality of life. Once confined to large cities, graffiti now appears in small towns and rural areas across the nation. Some graffiti can be removed or painted over, but it is likely to reappear almost immediately.

## Solution Development

The city of Paris approached the graffiti problem by erecting billboards in public places and allowing people to deface them at leisure. Paris, however, has never endured the amount of graffiti that has plagued U.S. cities. Billboards might be worth a try in this country, but they seem unlikely to make a significant dent in this widespread problem.

A more lasting solution would be to modify all spray paint so that it will not adhere to metal, brick, and stone surfaces.

## Solution Delivery Method

Those of you who want to solve this problem might use a *high-technology* SDM. You would start by developing a chemical substance that could be sprayed onto buildings, monuments, and vehicles in order to prevent vandals' paint from adhering to the surfaces. Graffiti could then be easily washed off as soon as it appeared.

Once this high-tech product is in place, you could develop another paint-resistant substance to be used in the manufacture of metal, bricks, and concrete so that vehicles and structures made of these materials would remain graffiti-free from the beginning.

These two products could be sold like other industrial components and could also be marketed to government agencies, school systems, construction companies, and vehicle manufacturers.

## BANKRUPT U.S. FARM SYSTEM

### Problem Formulation

The U.S. farm system is suffering from very low corn, wheat, and grain prices—so low that farmers lose money on every sale—at a time when half the population of the world goes to bed hungry each night. Government interference has confused the market for farm products and complicated potential solutions. President Jimmy Carter's retaliatory embargo on wheat shipments to the U.S.S.R., for example, served only to cause the Soviet Union to buy its grain from Argentina rather than from the United States.

The failure of the farm system has a domino effect on the U.S. economy, since it causes financial disaster for farm-equipment suppliers, banks, and merchants in farming communities.

## Solution Development

Conglomerate logic—so successful in American industry in the 1960s and 1970s—should be applied to the farm system. This logic states that if cash flow slows down in one crop, the farmer who is part of a farming conglomerate can rely on cash flow from another crop. Instead of riding up and down with changing market trends, members of a conglomerate cut through the cycles and ride a smoother path. It has worked in industry, and we can assume it would work in farming as well.

## Solution Delivery Method

In this instance, you would choose the *leveraged buy-out* SDM to form a conglomerate of farms of different sorts and in different areas. You might, for example, acquire a mixture of corn farms, dairy farms, cattle spreads, and truck farms. By doing this, you would be able to economize in purchasing seeds and farm equipment, and at the same time achieve diversity across a number of crops. You could introduce other industrial techniques as well, including equity incentives, central purchasing, pension plans, central borrowing and recruiting, and training programs.

# LOW READING SCORES

## Problem Formulation

Many U.S. public schools have failed to teach children to read. Large numbers of students receive high school diplomas despite the fact that they are functionally illiterate. They face the prospect of minimum-wage jobs or unemployment, and some of them turn to crime.

## Solution Development

A number of studies have demonstrated that students retain as much as five times more information when they receive computer-assisted instruction (CAI) in addition to conventional classroom teaching. The entrepreneur could address the reading problem by finding a way to put personal computers in front of students with a high potential for illiteracy. This solution has been discussed for many years, and there have been many attempts to introduce CAI to schools. However, many of these attempts have been top down. The entrepreneurial process is bottom up.

*PERT: Low Reading Scores*

| Months: | 1 | 2 | 3 | 4 | 5 |
|---|---|---|---|---|---|
| Finances: | Meet with family, friends; begin writing business plan | Raise family funds; complete, submit business plan to computer dealers | | | |
| Service: | | | | | |
| Facilities and equipment: | Use dining room table | | | Computer dealers provide demo PCs, projections, education software | |
| People: | | | | Enlist volunteer help of children | |
| | | | | Train children to use software during presentations | |
| Administration: | | | | | Complete training—use scripts if necessary; establish sales force objectives, compensation, territories |
| Marketing: | Write mission sheet, "welcome to our company" | Revise promo literature; meet with low-priced computer companies; (e.g., Atari) | Negotiate with Atari, Commodore, Radio Shack | Sign interim contracts with computer companies | Seek endorsements from PTAs; meet with teachers |

| Months: | 6 | 7 | 8 | 9 | 10 |
|---|---|---|---|---|---|
| Finances: | Computer dealers finance starter kits, training | | | | Collect broker's fee for equipment sale |
| Service: | | Teacher's home used for first beta test of products | Computer party and additional beta tests | First additional parties; complete beta tests | Additional parties; unsupervised tests |
| Facilities and equipment: | Computer dealers prepare starter kits | Computer dealers provide facilities, equipment, instructions for teachers | Computer dealers provide facilities, equipment, instructions; look for office | Computer dealers provide facilities, equipment; rent office | |
| People: | Hire secretary, bookkeeper | Interview sales manager (former teacher, chapter chairperson) | Additional interviews | Hire sales manager | Interview chief administrative officer |
| Administration: | | Teachers (no computer consultants) purchase territories, kits; consultant training | Additional consultants purchase territories, kits; additional training | Additional recruiting | |
| Marketing: | Make presentations at faculty conferences, district meetings | Make additional presentations; debug presentations | Make additional presentations | First equipment sale to a school district | |

## PERT: *Low Reading Scores* (Continued)

| Months: | 11 | 12 | 13 | 14 | 15 |
|---|---|---|---|---|---|
| Finances: | | | | | |
| Service: | | | | | |
| Facilities and equipment: | Additional parties | Additional parties Decide on second office location | Additional parties Look for second office | Additional parties Rent second office | Additional parties |
| People: | Additional interviews; promote consultants to salespersons | Hire chief administrative officer; interview office–directors, sales manager | Additional interviews | Hire office-sales manager, secretary | Make promotions, (i.e., sales manager to regional sales manager) |
| Administration: | Sales directors begin assisting in recruiting, training | Establish financial control officer | | | |
| Marketing: | Make additional presentations | Make additional presentations; secure national contracts with computer companies | Second equipment sale to a school district | Repeat procedures in new city; meet with PTAs, teachers, district boards | |

| Months: | 16 | 17 | 18 | 19 | 20 | 21 |
|---|---|---|---|---|---|---|
| Finances: | | | | | | |
| Service: | Additional parties | Additional parties | Additional parties | Additional parties | Additional parties | Additional parties |
| Facilities and equipment: | Decide on third office location | Look for third office | Rent third office | Decide on fourth office location | Look for fourth office | Rent fourth office |
| People: | Interview additional office-sales manager, marketing vice president | Additional interviews | Hire office-sales manager, secretary, marketing vice president | Make additional promotions (i.e., regional sales manager to national sales manager) | Interview additional office-sales manager | Hire office-sales manager, secretary |
| Administration: | | | | | | |
| Marketing: | | Obtain PR in national press | | Publish improved reading scores in *New York Times* | | |

## Solution Delivery Method

A low-cost SDM would be *franchise on OPA*, where the OPA is the training facilities of large computer dealers such as IBM, Sears, and Computerland coupled with a *party plan* marketing SDM. Their motivation would be pro-active altruism: to demonstrate their concern for the children in the community. At the same time, the dealers would be creating potential customers for their computers. The community would provide word-of-mouth advertising and new customers for the store. Other advantages would include turning the teachers who use the training rooms into a party plan sales force. They could triple their income via after school marketing. PERT chart begins on page 172..

## LACK OF RETAIL STORES IN INNER CITIES

### Problem Formulation

Following the demonstrations and the riots that lit up the night skies in the early 1970s, many retail establishments vanished from inner cities, leaving great gaping holes in numerous communities. Some neighborhood supermarkets were burned out. The owners of other stores were scared out of the inner cities, and still others were boycotted out. Dry cleaners, hairdressers, coffee shop owners, and other merchants disappeared from the inner cities during those difficult years. They did not return, and no one came to fill in the gaps they left behind. Today, as a result, the residents of some city neighborhoods must ride a bus fifteen blocks or more to the nearest food market, drugstore, or barbershop.

### Solution Development

The federal government, through the Small Business Administration and other agencies, has attempted to remedy this situation in various ways, all of which have been top-down, and most of which have been unsuccessful. Throwing money at this problem has not made it go away. Grassroots solutions have had only spotty success. A few national franchises have opened stores in inner cities under the supervision of skilled and good-hearted managers. Some of these franchises have been successful; a few of them are showcases. But fried chicken is not the only product the people of the inner cities need.

This problem cries out for a classical entrepreneurial solution: transferring ownership of inner city establishments to the residents and simultaneously teaching them the business skills needed to operate them.

## Solution Delivery Method

An entrepreneurial company could obtain a *facilities management* contract from a city. The company would agree to turn burned-out or abandoned stores into bustling retail emporiums. Part of the ownership and all of the management of the stores would eventually be placed in the hands of area residents. The facilities-management company could retain some ownership, or it could participate in the revenues of the shops that it returns to financial health. It could pool the cash flow and multiply it via conventional leverage techniques.

The entrepreneur could send people out to interview area residents for the purpose of determining which individuals would be most likely to succeed as small-business people and merchants. The facilities-management company could then train the potential business people in bookkeeping, business law, marketing, and other management functions. Then franchisors would be invited to demonstrate their franchising schemes to the business-owners-in-training.

The entrepreneurial company would raise capital or take out loans from responsible corporations that are sensitive to the urban community's need to bootstrap its way out of poverty. These funds would be invested in the small businesses and used to purchase franchises or as working capital to launch small businesses. The entrepreneurial company would provide management consulting and financial mentoring to the small-business people until they gained sound footing.

Eventually, with fifty or sixty franchises in its portfolio and retaining perhaps twenty-five percent ownership of each plus consulting fees and facilities-management contracts, the entrepreneurial company could conceivably achieve revenues of $3 million in its flagship city. At that point—or even before that point—it could replicate itself in other cities. With expansion into ten cities, the company could show revenues of $30 million and a healthy bottom line.

In addition to the profits it could earn, the entrepreneurial company would be helping hundreds of thousands of people to lead better, richer lives—in other words, it would be acting altruistically; it would be giving. What better means could one find to help one's neighbors?


# HIGH COST OF SOCIAL SECURITY

## Problem Formulation

The single largest component of the trillion dollar U.S. federal budget is the Social Security System. In addition to gobbling up cash, this system contributes to inflation. When people receive payment but do not recip-rocate by helping to produce goods or services, the result is more money in circulation, which drives the price of goods and services up.

A secondary problem of the Social Security System, as pointed out by George Gilder in *Wealth & Poverty* (New York: Basic Books, 1981) is the moral hazard common to all insurance systems. Moral hazard is the risk that a policy will encourage the behavior or promote the disaster that it insures against. Malpractice suits, for example, are "encouraged" by the existence of malpractice insurance. Arson is a response to the availability of fire insurance. Similarly, according to Martin Feldstein, former chair-man of the Council of Economic Advisors, a decline in savings is a response to the rise in retirement benefits. It is perhaps for this reason that the rate of savings in the United States is one-third that of England and half that of France.

In short, the Social Security System is expensive; it contributes to inflation; it encourages older people to be unproductive; and it results in a tendency *not* to save money for the future.

## Solution Development

The insurance industry in the United States grew up with the nation in the nineteenth century. It began by insuring against the destruction of cargoes during transport and by insuring the lives of the settlers who left the coastal port cities to make their way across this continent to isolated and treacherous frontiers.

Private insurance remained very much a part of entrepreneurial America until the mid-1930s. Before 1935, in fact, more than half of all welfare payments came from private charities. By contrast, in 1980 private charities contributed less than one percent of all such payments. Similarly, before the establishment of the Social Security System, many children cared for their parents throughout old age. Now, as George Gilder points out, many aging parents have to contribute financial help to their children, who are burdened with the constantly increasing Social Security tax.

The Social Security System offers few measurable benefits, but it does have a negative effect on self-reliance and on the motivation to work and to save. As this nation again becomes an entrepreneurial society, its Social Security System should be transferred from public to private stewardship.

## Solution Delivery Method

As a first step, the present Social Security administration should be run by an entrepreneurial company under a *facilities management* contract.

The entrepreneurial company could, with predictable ease, bid ninety-five percent of the current SSA budget and be confident of operating the system at a five percent profit after saving the government five percent. Once in charge of managing the system, the entrepreneur would almost certainly find, among other bureaucratic excesses, a tremendous number of unneeded employees and an oversupply of computers, desks, file cabinets, typewriters, telephones, and rented property. The trimming could start right there.

Insurance company executives with the entrepreneurial spirit could be pulled together into one start-up company using equity to raise enough capital to buy insurance policies from the U.S. government. The government might guarantee the loans to the start-up company, as it does with federally backed mortgages, thus making the paper salable. The financing of the Social Security System would, however, return to private hands.

The entrepreneurial company could then redesign the system from top to bottom, in the process creating an actuarially based insurance organization. This newly reorganized system would levy a Social Security tax only on those people who have made no provision for their old age; individuals who have saved sufficient funds or contributed to private pension plans would not be taxed. In addition, people over age sixty-five who desire to continue working would be allowed to defer receiving their benefits for as long as they wished. This would prevent people from becoming unproductive sooner than necessary, increase the size of the fund available for the truly needy, and reduce the amount of the tax paid by productive people.

The SSA facilities manager could be persuasive with the entrepreneurial heads of other industries, encouraging them to make significant charitable contributions and to invest their pension funds in the venture capital-entrepreneurial process. This would further lighten the burden of caring for the needy, most of which is now borne by productive people.

## LACK OF AFFORDABLE HIGH-QUALITY DAY CARE

### Problem Formulation

Today some sixty percent of the women in the United States have jobs. A large number of these working women have children young enough to require care during all or part of the workday. High-quality day care is difficult to find and in many cases extremely expensive.

The federal government attempted to solve this problem in the 1970s by funding day-care centers for the children of working women, but almost all of those facilities closed as a result of incompetence or misappropriation of funds, or both. Private day-care centers have enjoyed some modest successes, but their numbers have begun to dwindle in the wake of the child-abuse cases of recent years, which have made liability insurance hard to get.

## Solution Development

Those who think in entrepreneurial terms will realize that female employees will be more productive and reliable if they are sure that their children are in good hands during the day. Surely the opposite would be true of the woman who is constantly worried about the welfare of her child or who must often stay home from work because her child's caretaker didn't show up. In this situation the entrepreneur will see that employers have a responsibility to address the day-care problem and to seek solutions to it.

## Solution Delivery Method

Two SDMs can be combined to effectively deliver a solution to this problem. They are *facilities management* and *franchising*. In this instance, however, instead of presenting a theoretical solution, I'm going to relate the story of an entrepreneur who has actually put these two SDMs into action and come up with a satisfactory solution to the day-care problem.

Joan Barnes founded Gymboree Corporation in 1980 as a day-care facilities management company. She began by getting in touch with corporations that employed large numbers of women. Barnes contracted to manage the child care needs of those female employees, using the corporations' facilities and thus obviating the need to buy or rent suitable space. Gymboree Corporation soon had eight day-care centers up and running. At this point, Barnes's capacity for expansion was limited by the amount of time and the number of people she had at her disposal. Instead of stopping there, however, she began to sell franchises, at which point she hired a former Midas Muffler employee to head up Gymboree's franchising division. This move allowed her company to continue growing rapidly *before* it attracted serious copycat competitors.

The day-care company now employs twenty-four people and has several million dollars in revenues. Housewives and part-time or former teachers are trained to run the Gymboree centers, which offer traditional day-care activities for pre-school children: fingerpainting, exercise, play-learning experiences, a nap, and lunch. Some of the managers eventually buy their own franchises.

Barnes claims to know little about business, but she does understand the entrepreneurial spirit. Here's what she has to say about it: "It's sort of like jumping off a boat and the alligators begin to follow you; you bet you'll learn to swim real quick. . . . But if you stand out on the dock and say, 'Now, there's an alligator in the water, and I'm never going to get across,' then you never will get across. . . . You just have to get into the water and work it out."

## CANCER TREATMENT

### Problem Formulation

Cancer is the second largest killer in the United States after heart attack. Approximately 350,000 people are stricken each year in the United States with breast, lung, and thoracic cancer; and an additional 2,000 people are living with these cancers on a residual basis at any one time. The present means of treating these and other cancers are chemotherapy, radiation therapy, and surgery. These treatments are 30 percent effective.

### Solution Development

There exists another form of treatment known as photodynamic therapy, or PDT, which has been approximately 70 percent effective with these forms of cancer and certain others at Roswell Park Memorial Hospital, Buffalo, New York; Ohio State Medical Center, Columbus, Ohio; the Mayo Clinic, Rochester, Minnesota; and in Japan. Because the Food and Drug Administration requires extensive testing prior to the marketing of a new drug to the general public, PDT is being used in the United States on a clinical trial basis for terminally ill patients only. In Japan, however, PDT can be the treatment of choice.

### Solution Delivery Method

There is an entrepreneurial opportunity to introduce PDT more broadly and rapidly, and with FDA approval. PDT involves injecting a drug into the bloodstream. The drug, known as hemataporphorin derivative, is selectively taken up by the tumor cells and washes out of the healthy cells several hours later. When light is then put on the tumor, it is killed. The aftereffect is sunburn; avoidance of strong sunlight for forty-eight hours after treatment is recommended. The treatment is neither toxic nor painful, and it can be done profitably for around $1,000.

This solution method is a *high technology* launch: produce a stable compound, obtain the rights from the FDA to test it, and sell it to oncologists for use in the treatment of some of their patients. With as much speed as possible, gather sufficient data to convince the FDA to approve the treatment for direct marketing to oncologists for use as a primary treatment against lung, breast, and thoracic cancer.

There are no simple solutions to these large problems, and it is not clear that they are completely soluble by means of the entrepreneurial process. However, if the law of reciprocity is the principal force in causing certain people to attempt to solve the problems of others, then entrepreneurial gift-giving is what we should look to as the method for removing or mitigating society's largest problems. And who are society's gift-givers? Its entrepreneurs. It is they who understand and appeal to the wants and needs of others and, in so doing, promote the effective operation of markets. They are society's altruists.

# 9

# *Step-by-Step Entrepreneurial Launch Plan*

In order to launch your entrepreneurial company in the most effective way, you should follow an orderly progression of events, which we will call the *launch plan*. Here are the twelve steps in that launch plan:

1. Formulate the problem
2. Develop the solution to the problem
3. Select the solution delivery method
4. Create a PERT chart
5. Write a business plan
6. Create a prototype of your solution and protect it with a patent or copyright, if necessary
7. Beta-test your solution
8. Debug the solution and modify your business plan
9. Begin production in small volumes
10. Hire a corporate achiever
11. Raise the necessary venture capital
12. Begin full production and marketing

To avoid losing time, wasting capital, and compromising your credibility, you should follow these twelve steps *in order.* If you scramble them, you are likely to end up with an unsuccessful launch. Suppose, for example, that you develop a solution (2), write a business plan (5), and raise venture capital (11), but you fail to take the other steps. You'll land in the market with a product that hasn't been prototyped, tested, or debugged, and your chances of succeeding will be almost nonexistent. Take your time. Don't try to burst into the marketplace by means of brute force, because that just doesn't work.

In this final chapter, I'll take you through these twelve crucial steps one at a time, explaining each move and giving examples to clarify certain points. As you head into your own entrepreneurial launch, return to this chapter as often as you need to in order to stay on the safe path to entrepreneurial success.

## FORMULATE THE PROBLEM

This is the most creative aspect of the entrepreneurial launch. It requires you to analyze the problem that you have chosen to solve, studying it from various angles. You can accomplish this most effectively by asking yourself a number of questions:

- Are people aware of the problem?
- Do they know the cost to them of the problem?
- Is the problem equally severe and costly to all of them? Most of them? None of them?
- Is the problem discussed in a newsletter, a trade journal, newspapers, or television?
- Is the problem common to a widespread geographic area?
- Do people who have the problem customarily buy solutions from entrepreneurs? From consultants? From large companies?
- Do people who have the problem attend seminars or industry-wide conferences where solutions and new ideas are discussed, or do they wait for solutions to come to them?
- Is there a trade association or any other institutional barrier that mitigates the flow of new ideas into this marketplace?
- Will this product need to be accompanied by a service or instruction?

## DEVELOP THE SOLUTION TO THE PROBLEM

What you do at this stage of the launch will depend in part on the sort of problem and solution you have chosen. If you are working on a high-tech start-up, for example, you will now seek and hire a scientific team to help you develop your product. If you have chosen a consumer product or capital equipment solution, now is the time either to assemble a product development group or to license the right to produce and market a product someone else has developed.

Whatever solution you have chosen, you should at this point standardize your solution so as to make it useful to the largest possible number of people. Also, if your product is to contain a component that must occasionally be replaced—like the blade in a razor or the ribbon in an office machine—spend some time right now developing replacement parts that are efficient, reasonably priced, and easy to install.

Keep going over the DEJ factors. Analyze your solution from every possible angle, always remembering that it will be successful *only* if it has as many DEJ factors as possible—preferably all eight of them.

## SELECT THE SOLUTION DELIVERY METHOD

Now ask yourself exactly what kind of business this should be. In other words, choose your solution delivery method. Go back through Chapter 7, where the SDMs are listed and explained. Study them until you are certain which one will be right for your solution. Use the following list for quick reference:

1. Facilities management
2. Prepaid subscription
3. Franchising
4. Party plan
5. Celebrity-endorsed consumer product
6. Consumer product
7. High technology
8. Cookie cutter
9. Capital equipment
10. Tollgate
11. Newsletter-seminar
12. Franchise on OPA

You may decide to combine several SDMs into one business plan, especially if you are an information or franchise entrepreneur. For example, newsletters are usually marketed on a prepaid subscription basis; franchising chains occasionally rely on celebrity endorsement.

## CREATE A PERT CHART

The word "PERT," as I mentioned earlier, is an acronym for "program evaluation and review tool." Using the PERTs in the preceding chapter as your model, diagram all of the steps in your business launch, plotting each move against a time frame and keeping the tasks organized into categories such as finances, facilities and equipment, and product. Assign a cost to each activity, and include all twelve launch steps in your PERT.

Schedule each move carefully, taking time to consider the worst-case scenario for each step. Remember that if one event—say, developing the prototype—takes two months longer than you planned, your company will need additional capital to cover rent, salaries, and other expenses for those extra eight weeks.

PERT charting will encourage you to temper your optimism with "downside planning." This healthful exercise consists of continually asking yourself a question: "Now, if this move backfires, what can I do to repair the damage or cover the shortfall?"

## WRITE A BUSINESS PLAN

Your objective here is to take the skeleton of a PERT and put flesh on it by adding descriptive material, which will include detailed financial information. Your PERT plots events against time, and each of those events will cost a certain amount of money. Revenues and cost of goods sold will at some point begin to appear. The result will be a cash flow projection of thirty-six to sixty months. Figure 9.1 shows you how to diagram this flow numerically and graphically.

The key considerations in preparing a business plan are as follows:

1. The components of revenue
2. The components of variable costs
3. The components of fixed costs

These components are a function of the events of the launch process that you have developed up to this point.

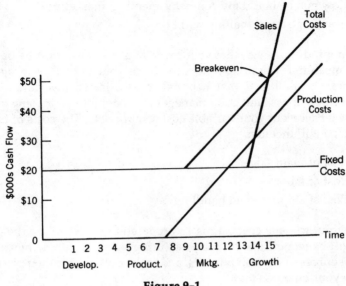

**Figure 9-1.**

The components of revenue include:

1. Sales—cash, installment, or terms
2. Rental—down payment, terms, bankability
3. Fees collected
4. Service income collected and contractual
5. Peripheral sales—ratio to primary sale
6. Meter income
7. Royalties collected

You can make a revenue projection by asking yourself the following questions:

1. How many units can I expect each representative to sell each month?
2. Can my company gradually build up its sales to five percent of the total market?
3. What is the experience curve of other companies that are similar to mine?

4. How much should my company spend on marketing?
5. How large a test mailing will I need?

Keep in mind, however, that your revenue projections must be based on valid, meaningful assumptions; otherwise your cash flow projections will lack credibility. If that happens, sophisticated investors will not back your business, and good managers will not join your company.

Now let's look at your variable cost components. The costs of production alone will include:

1. Cost of materials
2. Cost of labor
3. Cost of shipping and handling

It is helpful to have cost estimates prepared or reviewed by the person who will be responsible for manufacturing. Also, be sure to locate alternative sources of key components, and make certain that their prices will fit into your business plan.

In addition to your production costs, you will have to bear the variable cost components of selling and marketing. The costs of selling will include support and commission for all or some of the following employees:

1. Direct sales representatives
2. Marketing representatives
3. Dealers
4. Franchisees
5. Party-plan representatives

Your variable marketing costs will be spread among these functions:

1. Advertising
2. Direct mail
3. Public relations
4. Consultants

Depending on the nature of your entrepreneurial company, you may have additional variable cost components.

The fixed cost components of your business will most likely include;

1. Management salaries, FICA, and benefits
2. Administrators' salaries, FICA, and benefits

3. Insurance
4. Legal fees
5. Accounting
6. Rent
7. Office equipment
8. Office and plant furnishings
9. Utilities
10. Telephone
11. Sanitation
12. Factory overhead
13. Shrinkage
14. Postage
15. Stationery and consumables

A credible basis for these costs is as important as for any other. Attention to detail is one of the most prized skills of successful entrepreneurs.

Do your business plan projections by hand. Do not use a software package. The old-fashioned method will result in a more thorough understanding of the business plan. When it is finished, ask your board of advisers or directors to evaluate it.

## CREATE AND PROTECT YOUR PROTOTYPE

### The Product Prototype

If your solution is a product, you must at this point design, build, and assemble a *prototype*—an original model on which all others will be fashioned. As soon as you have accomplished this, you should patent your device. A patent attorney can help you file the necessary materials with the U.S. Patent Office. The patent is absolutely vital if you wish to prevent others from infringing on your right to the exclusive use of your idea. You may wish to introduce complications into your patent application in order to make your device difficult for others to copy. *Do not go public with your product until you have filed with the Patent Office.*

### Service and Information Prototypes

If your solution is a service, you will have to describe it in complete detail in a manual. You may wish to obfuscate it a bit so as to make it difficult for imitators to copy. When you are satisfied with your description, get it into copyright by filing it with the U.S. Copyright Office. Again, the services of an attorney will be useful here.

If your solution is information, it should be described in elaborate detail in a manual and then copyrighted like the service solution.

## BETA TEST YOUR SOLUTION

When you have created your product or service, you should test it thoroughly in your plant or office to see (1) if it works and (2) if it is innovative. These are known as *alpha tests*.

The *beta tests* are conducted outside your plant or office. A beta test involves putting your solution into the hands of potential consumers and letting them use it. The most common type of beta test is probably the focus group. For this test, you simply assemble a group of potential customers in a conference room or in someone's home. Put the product into their hands, show them how to use it, and then watch them and listen to what they say about your solution. This way you can find out what they think of these aspects of your product:

- The name of your product or service
- The packaging and general appearance
- Its price
- The directions that come with the product
- Its usefulness
- The way it feels in their hands
- The degree of ease with which it can be operated
- How well it does what it's supposed to do

Decide ahead of time what you want to learn through your beta tests. Choose your focus groups and your meeting places so as to be sure of getting the information you need. You may want to offer your beta testers a discount on future purchases in return for testing your product.

If your solution is a magazine or newsletter, you can beta test it by preparing a dummy issue that includes a questionnaire. Mail copies to a small target audience, and ask people to fill in the questionnaire and return it to you. Spend a good deal of time formulating the questionnaire so that the respondents' answers will tell you what you need to know about their opinion of the issue.

## DEBUG THE SOLUTION AND MODIFY YOUR BUSINESS PLAN

Chances are, the beta tests will turn up one or more weaknesses in your solution. If so, your next step is to debug your product or service—in other words, correct any weaknesses and rebuild or rewrite the solution so as to incorporate any necessary changes. Once you've done that, you'll need to run a second wave of beta tests on your debugged product.

When you finally get your solution into working condition, you'll need to modify your business plan to reflect all changes, cost differences, and delays. The modified business plan—which, by the way, might have to be revised many times—will become your company's strategy. You'll use it to hire key managers, and you'll show it to banks and other sources of capital.

This is a good time to put your company's *mission* in writing. Do this by stating the ultimate purpose of the business, its reason for being. This is also the time to formulate your company's *ethical standards*. How will customers be treated? What kind of behavior will not be tolerated—drug abuse, sexism, racism, taking credit for other people's ideas? What attitudes will be encouraged? And so forth.

## BEGIN PRODUCTION IN SMALL VOLUMES

At this stage you need to put your production system into operation, not so much to turn out goods as to gain information about the production process. Here are just a few of the things you'll be looking for at this stage:

- How good is the production team? Are they adequately trained? Do they work well together?
- What problems, if any, are likely to crop up in the mass-production process?
- How good are the suppliers? Will the production process be slowed down because of delayed delivery of supplies? How many alternative suppliers are available?
- Are raw materials in abundant supply? How many alternate sources are available?
- What kind of quality-control mechanism works best for this particular production team?

Depending on the nature of your solution, you may have to add to or subtract from the list. Compile a detailed list of things you want to learn from this small-volume production process. During this stage, make whatever adjustments seem necessary to achieve the most efficient and satisfactory production operation.

## HIRE A CORPORATE ACHIEVER

At this point you are ready to choose a corporate achiever or a business partner to manage your company. This person must already have demonstrated a high level of ability in the corporate world, preferably in a field related to the one your new company is about to enter. He or she should possess skills that complement your own. For example, if you are a highly creative, high-energy person, the corporate achiever should be thorough and meticulous.

Don't make the mistake of hiring someone who is less capable than you are or who lacks the strength of character to stand up to you when he or she believes you are wrong. Try to find someone who is as courageous, intelligent, and capable as you are.

Your business partner should review the business plan and modify it as necessary, with your guidance. You may call on the corporate achiever to support the plan before commercial banks and venture capitalists.

In most instances, corporate achievers are older than entrepreneurs and more conservative. They usually have greater personal assets to protect, and they may be more meticulous in dress, speech, and demeanor. Their reasons for joining an entrepreneurial company should include a desire to build something, to become a member of a problem-solving organization, and to regain their sense of purpose. The glue that binds them to the entrepreneur is equity—a piece of the action.

## RAISE THE NECESSARY VENTURE CAPITAL

It is possible, though unlikely, that this step will not apply to your entrepreneurial company. There are, after all, a good many businesses that don't require venture capital or that need an amount so small that it can be raised through family and friends. Or, in the case of a multiple-SDM company, you may be able to get started with customer financing only. If you're one of the lucky entrepreneurs who can do without venture capital, feel free to breeze right on past this step.

If you do need to raise capital, however, get it without delay. You will need it to fill the cash flow deficit that is going to show up when you prepare your marketing cash flow sheet. Keep a sharp eye out for changes in your need for capital. You may have to adjust the total amount needed each time you run into a delay or make a change in your production schedule.

## BEGIN FULL PRODUCTION AND MARKETING

At this point you are ready to roll out your product or service, to give your entrepreneurial gift to the audience whose problem you have set out to solve. If you have taken care to complete every step in the entrepreneurial process to the best of your considerable ability, your launch will be a success.

During the roll-out, you'll want to keep in mind a list of tips from a truly successful entrepreneur, Roy H. Park. His company, Park Communications, Inc., established in 1962, owns and operates seventy different publications and broadcasting properties. In 1976, he delivered a speech at Cornell University's Graduate School of Business and Public Administration. Here are his roll-out suggestions:

1. Pay attention to details
2. Get things done on time
3. Delegate to others the tasks that they handle as well as or better than you do
4. Use showmanship and imagination to dramatize what you are doing
5. Take action, if you have the facts and common sense and if you move, you've got better than a fifty percent chance of being right
6. Do your business homework
7. Reinvest the cash flow as it is generated—but always keep a liquid position

Now, at the end of this discussion of entrepreneurship, you *do* have the facts, and chances are you have common sense as well. This, then, is the time to move.

I wish you luck.

# Index